BEAM, STRAIGHT UP

The Bold Story of the First Family of Bourbon

FRED NOE

with

JIM KOKORIS

WILEY

John Wiley & Sons, Inc.

Cover image: Matt Barton
Cover design: Paul McCarthy

Published by John Wiley & Sons, Inc., Hoboken, New Jersey.
Published simultaneously in Canada.

For general information on our other products and services or for technical support, please contact our Customer Care Department within the United States at (800) 762-2974, outside the United States at (317) 572-3993 or fax (317) 572-4002.

Wiley publishes in a variety of print and electronic formats and by print-on-demand. Some material included with standard print versions of this book may not be included in e-books or in print-on-demand. If this book refers to media such as a CD or DVD that is not included in the version you purchased, you may download this material at http://booksupport.wiley.com. For more information about Wiley products, visit www.wiley.com.

Library of Congress Cataloging-in-Publication Data:

Noe, Fred.
  Beam, straight up : the bold story of the first family of bourbon / Fred Noe and Jim Kokoris.
    p. cm.
  Includes index.
  ISBN 978-1-118-37836-6 (cloth); ISBN 978-1-118-43813-8 (ebk);
  ISBN 978-1-118-43815-2 (ebk); ISBN 978-1-118-43810-7 (ebk)
    1. James B. Beam Distilling Company—History. 2. Noe, Fred.
    3. Beam, James B., 1864-1947—Family. 4. Distillers—United States—Biography.
    5. Whiskey industry—United States—History. I. Kokoris, Jim. II. Title.
  HD9395.U47J366 2012
  338.7'663522092273—dc23   2012026256

Printed in the United States of America
10 9 8 7 6 5 4 3 2 1

To my family, past, present, and future.

CONTENTS

CONTENTS

PROLOGUE

When they first asked me to write a book about my life, I wasn't too keen on the idea. I'm not big on books, haven't read as many as I probably should. Besides, I wasn't sure I had that much to say. But the more I thought about it, the more I warmed to the idea. I guess my life's as interesting as some, so why not?

Now, there've been books written about bourbon before. There've even been books written about my family and the company that they built, Beam Inc. So rather than go over subjects that have been covered, I thought I'd offer a little bit of everything: the history of the Jim Beam family and my memories of growing up in it; the history of bourbon and how it's made; and the things I've learned from being the master distiller and ambassador of one of the world's most recognizable brands, Jim Beam® Bourbon. And, just in case you're thinking of starting your own business, I added my views, thoughts, and recommendations—free of charge—on how build a brand and a company for the long haul. I think I have a little insight into that, considering we're more than 200 years old.

I guess in the end, this book is part entertainment, part educational, and maybe, just maybe a little inspirational. So sit back and pour yourself a drink. I had a big time writing this thing; hopefully you'll have just as big a time reading it.

—Fred Noe,
Jim Beam's great-grandson and
Master Distiller and Global Bourbon
Ambassador of Beam Inc.

FOREWORD

I like things honest and real. That's why I like Fred Noe and the Jim Beam family. No pretensions, no smoke and mirrors, no posturing or posing. Just straightforward people, making a straightforward whiskey.

When I heard Fred was working on a book, my first thought was, "It's about time." He has stories to tell: about his family, particularly his larger-than-life father, Booker; about the whiskey he makes, which I'm proud to be sponsored by; and about himself. I've known Fred for years; he's a natural entertainer—he's lived the life—and this book is pure entertainment.

It's also educational, offering its fair share of history. For more than 200 years, the Beam family has been part of our culture, the quintessential American company. Started on the frontier in the foothills of the Appalachians, it grew while our country grew. For seven generations the Beams persevered, making whiskey enjoyed by presidents, Civil War generals, musicians, writers, but most important, everyday people. For seven generations they've put their special craft first and worked hard at keeping a proud tradition alive: Jim Beam Bourbon, an American icon, known the world over.

So here's to Fred and the Beams. Pioneers, artists, craftsmen, scientists—whiskey rock 'n' rollers no doubt!

And here's to a *great* book.

Cheers,
Kid Rock

1

A LITTLE HISTORY

I was born on March 9, 1957, in the Baptist Hospital in Louisville, Kentucky. At first, my grandfather, my mother's father, refused to come see me because he was a serious Catholic and didn't like the idea of me being born in a place where you could eat meat on Fridays. But he eventually came and we all went home in a brand new 1957 Ford Fairlane that my dad, Booker, bought just for the occasion. My dad said his son was coming home in style, so he ran his bank account down to $21 to buy that car, which was kind of a waste because I don't remember that drive at all. But Booker had a flair for the dramatic, so that's how I arrived in

Bardstown, Kentucky, the Bourbon Capital of the World, a seventh-generation, soon-to-be whiskey-making Beam.

That's the official, birth-certificate beginning of my story, but my story really starts a lot earlier—way back around 1790. That's when—sit down now, this might take a while—my great-great-great-great-grandfather Jacob Beam crossed over into Kentucky from Maryland through the Cumberland Gap with his wife, Mary. Jacob was of German descent; his name was originally spelled "Boehm" and he, like a lot of people, was pushing westward, looking for a place he could put down roots, make a life.

He found that place near Hardin Creek in what's now Washington County in central Kentucky. It was a nice tract of land, about 100 acres, close to good streams and rivers, and he went to work on it right away. Germans like to work. Work is fun for them. So he went at it hard, raising hogs, cattle, horses, and tobacco, but mostly corn. Corn was king in Kentucky back then. The hot summers, the warmer winters, and spring water made it a perfect place for growing it. They grew a lot of it. Probably too much, so they turned some of that corn into whiskey, which was pretty common thing to do on the frontier. A lot of people knew how to do it. Making liquor was the safest and cheapest way to use up the extra corn because it was easy to transport downriver and wasn't susceptible to mildew. Using a water-driven mill to grind the corn and a pot still he had brought with him, Jacob slowly began making whiskey from a fermented mash of corn, rye, and malt.

The water he used was sweet Kentucky limestone—especially good for whiskey making since it's rich in calcium, which works well with yeast cells during the fermenting stage. (I promise, that's about as technical as I will get right now.)

Jacob tried different grain mixtures—a little more corn, a little less rye, a little more rye, a little less corn, back and forth, back and forth—until he hit on a new recipe in the mid-1790s. Bingo, he got it right. We still use that recipe today, keep it under lock and key.

He brought his first whiskey to market in 1795, and he entered a somewhat crowded marketplace. There was competition; a lot of people were making whiskey, even George Washington. Yes, *that* George Washington. He had a still over at Mount Vernon and records show that he turned a tidy little profit making rum and then, later, rye whiskey. (Washington was actually a fan of whiskey, especially during the Revolutionary War. In *The Book of Bourbon and Other Fine American Whiskeys*, my friend Gary Regan wrote that old George thought America should build a lot of distilleries, claiming that "the benefits arising from the moderate use of strong liquor have been experienced in all armies and are not to be disputed.")

But Jacob's whiskey stood out from the rest and it soon earned a following. People in Kentucky started talking about it, making special trips out to Hardin Creek to get it. They came on Sunday after church, came in the evening after the mules were tired and plowing was done, came before a wedding or on the way to a funeral. Tired and thirsty pioneers, looking for a little relief after another hard day at the office. After a while, his whiskey started to gain a following and its reputation, like Jacob's, grew throughout Kentucky and then through the Ohio River Valley. Old Jake's whiskey, top-shelf stuff, come and get it—it's worth the trip.

It's important to remember that up until that time, the whiskey that Jacob made was a novelty. New stuff. When people drank, they usually drank rum, which they made from sugar and molasses that was brought in from the Caribbean. They also made brandy from peaches and other fruits. Those spirits were popular in New England and consequently, the rest of Young America. So when Jake's whiskey came on the scene, it was something different, something special: liquor made from grains, particularly corn.

A lot of people and families lay claim to being the first to make bourbon or age it in oak barrels. Since records were scarce back then in Kentucky (pioneers were more interested in staying alive than trying to get legal patents on products and processes), no one is really sure who first hit on bourbon. I do know one thing for sure, though: while we definitely weren't the first family to make it, we definitely were the best.

After a while, Jacob had himself a pretty good little business, and he worked hard at it and it grew. Supply and demand. He had to keep up, and he did. Soon, he was shipping the whiskey out in oak barrels on flatboats, using the waterways. And he had a lot of water to work with.

Kentucky has more navigable streams and rivers than just about any state in the union, a real asset that Jake took advantage of. Some of his whiskey made it all the way to New Orleans and then to ports unknown.

His enterprise was growing and he needed help, so he brought in his son David, his 10th child (he had 12 children in all; he had a lot of energy), and together they worked the mill grinding the corn, and they worked the pot still, burning it off. After a few more years, Old Jake eventually called it quits and retired to another son's farm. Time to sit on the front porch. His job was done.

David Beam's job was just beginning. He threw himself into the business, and set it on a solid path. More and more distilleries were popping up all over Kentucky, and competition for what was now being called bourbon whiskey (named because it was made in what was then Bourbon County) was getting fierce. So, he ramped up production, made even more good use of the streams and rivers to ship it west and east, and all in all made a name for himself and the family. Things were pretty good.

They got better when his son David M. took over in 1853. Railroads were being built at a crazy pace; thousands and thousands of miles of track was being laid, and trains with steam engines were on the move. The trains, along with steamboats on the Mississippi, gave my family another and faster way to ship our product. The telegraph helped business too; when barkeepers ran low on whiskey, they had a way to reach distillers and order more.

Also adding to the growth of the industry was a change in the distilling process. David M. and other distillers were getting away from the pot still and using something called column stills. These new stills increased production so we could make more and more brown liquor.*

Thanks to these new distribution channels and processes, bourbon was proving popular, and it soon emerged as the drink of choice in the Old West. When cowboys bellied up to bars in frontier towns like Dodge City or San Antonio and asked for a whiskey, chances are they got bourbon. It was the cowboy drink.

During the Civil War, troops on both the Union and Confederate sides had their share of bourbon. After a battle, it helped eased their pain and fortify their spirits. It also served as a necessary anesthetic to help the wounded; medicines weren't what they are today. Kentucky was a

*Just in case you're interested, bourbon gets its dark color from sitting inside, or aging, in a new oak barrel that is burned or charred on the inside. When it comes off the still, it's white as water, and when it comes out of the barrel, it's brown, having absorbed the color of the caramelized layer of sugar that is created from the charring. That's some knowledge you can impress your friends with.

border state; it stayed in the Union. Mary Todd Lincoln, wife of the president of the Union, was from Kentucky, but you could still own slaves there, so it was about as close to being neutral as you could get. Legend has it that when the Union troops came through Bourbon County, the distilleries would fly the American flag; when the Confederates did, they flew the rebel colors. Both were good customers, no need to choose sides now.

General Ulysses Grant, commander of the Union forces, was probably the bourbon industry's biggest customer; he drank so much of it that congressmen started complaining to President Lincoln about him, said he was an embarrassment, wasn't fit to hold the position. Lincoln didn't care. Always a big Grant supporter, he reportedly responded, "Find out what he drinks and send a case to my other generals." (For the record, Grant drank Old Crow, which would one day become a fine Beam product.)

With demand for bourbon growing, David M. left the original distillery on Hardin Creek (his brother Joseph took it over) and founded a new one about seven miles west in Nelson County, near the new railroad. It was here that he launched a brand named Old Tub that would end up proving quite popular. He also brought his son into the enterprise. His name was Jim Beam. You probably have heard of him.

I never met my great-grandfather, so what I know is what I've been told, and I've been told a lot. He was only 16 when he went to work at the distillery and, along with his brother-in-law, Albert Hart, took it over when he was 30 years old, so he must have known what he was doing. (When I was 30, I was working the night shift on the bottling line, punching a clock.) I guess you could call him the Bill Gates of bourbon, because he took not just a business, but an entire industry, and kind of propelled it forward. He was the man all right.

From what I've been told, my great-grandfather was "classic Kentucky," a straightforward and simple man who saw things in black and white, threw big parties but probably didn't give too many toasts, and went to church but probably didn't sing too loud. He was a formal man, never went anywhere without a suit and tie—even fished and hunted in a suit and tie—and drove a Cadillac car back and forth from the distillery to Bardstown, a jug of family yeast sitting in the front seat next to him. That yeast was a Beam heirloom, passed down through the generations, and it turned the mash into alcohol. You see, you have to use the same yeast to keep your whiskey consistent and tasting right and he wasn't about to let it out of his sight. No room for error on that subject. My great-grandmother Mary, his wife, complained, said the yeast stunk up the house, said it smelled like old socks, but Jim didn't care. He just shrugged, asked what's for supper. That yeast was gold; it made his whiskey special and it smelled just fine to him.

According to an old newspaper we keep, *The Nelson County Register*, "Jim Beam was full of energy, no one was more popular than he." And by all accounts, that was true. Leslie Samuels, whose family would own the Maker's Mark distillery, was a next-door neighbor and a best friend. They were close, had big times together, and even had a special sidewalk put in to connect the two houses. They drank their share of whiskey out on the front porch together, discussing things: their hopes, ambitions, their dreams for life. One story about those two has stood the test of time, so I'll tell it now. Shows that my great-grandfather wasn't all work; he had himself a sense of humor too.

My great-grandmother Mary ("Maw Maw") Beam was a devout Catholic. Jim Beam wasn't. Anyway, the archbishop of the area, a higher-up to be sure, was coming to Bardstown for a visit. A big deal. Maw Maw Beam snapped into action, got the Big House and the entire town ready to receive him. She pulled out all the stops, had a parade planned, had a stage set up, put away the liquor in the basement. Then she dispatched Mr. Beam and Mr. Samuels to Louisville to pick him up while she waited at home for the Second Coming. Well, apparently when the two boys got to Louisville, they learned that the archbishop hadn't come. He was sick, stayed home in Chicago. (Archbishop or not, the guy could have called. But that's just my opinion. . . .) Anyway, Jim, who was a mason, and not wanting to disappoint the faithful back in Bardstown, especially his wife, decided to put on his Mason uniform, which included a hood that pretty much covered his whole face, get back in the convertible car they had come in, return to town, and take on the role of archbishop. They drove the parade route, waving to everyone and blessing people; they might have pulled over to take a few confessions, I'm not sure. When they got to the stage, Maw Maw was there to greet them, beaming with joy. She got the surprise of her life, though, when Jim took off his hood to reveal that rather than His Holiness, the town had just been genuflecting to a bourbon distiller. Everyone was shocked and confused, especially Maw Maw Beam, who, while not known for her temper, reportedly lost it on the stage and said a few very un-Christian things out loud. A bit of scene ensued in front of the whole town. I suspect Jim regretted his little stunt, but I'm glad he did it. It's made for a good story.

Down deep, parties and practical jokes aside, I don't think Jim Beam really cared if he was all that popular. What he really cared about was the family business. He wanted to grow it, he wanted to take it to a whole new level. And, by all accounts, he succeeded.

Like a lot of ambitious people, he had a single-minded purpose, a clear vision about how things should and were going to be, and nothing was going to get in his way. Eyes on the prize. Let me do my job, and you do yours. So, what's for supper?

By 1899, business was booming and demand was high. To accommodate it, he built new rack houses to store more whiskey, hired more people to do more work. Everything was going along about as well as could be. Things were moving forward.

Then, just like that, things stopped, stopped cold. The government decided that liquor was the root of all evil (though they later would decide it was the root of a lot of good tax revenue . . .) and declared that the production and sale of alcohol was illegal. Prohibition set in.

Now, to be fair, the bourbon industry knew Prohibition was coming. It wasn't like the federal government just sprang it on the country overnight. The temperance movement had been growing for decades, and individual states had already gone dry. But when something called the Volstead Act was passed in 1919, it still caught everyone in our business flat-footed, and the whiskey industry just shut down.

My great-grandfather did a lot of things to stay afloat during that time, but one thing he didn't do was go to jail. He sold the plant, took a few barrels home and stored them in his basement for his personal use, then locked up the barrels in the rack houses and decided to try his hand at some other ventures: operating a coal mine and then a rock quarry in Kentucky, and owning citrus groves in Florida. He was a duck out of water, though. Heart wasn't in it and it showed on his bottom line. Bourbon was in his blood, so he bid his time, waiting for the Repeal. He bought an old distillery, the Murphy Barber in Clermont, Kentucky, about 13 miles west of his old plant, and attached to that rock quarry. He and the family worked that quarry and waited for the storm to pass. The storm lasted a lot longer than he ever imagined, though. Thirteen years. Most distillers thought it would last five at most.

Now, a lot of people ask me about Prohibition, ask if we were in the bootlegging business, and they make a lot of assumptions when they do. They assume that we went into the business, that we kept making our whiskey on the sly, up in the hills. They romanticize the period. The truth is, I don't know exactly what took place during that time. It's not like we kept records on bootlegging or moonshining. I do know that when we shut down in 1920, we had a lot more bourbon in our rack houses than when we opened up some 13 years later. It went somewhere. Probably north, probably east. My cousin Carl Beam, who was a Master Distiller, said that he remembers seeing a line of shiny black cars outside the plant in the evenings with their trunks open. And the next morning, after those trunks were slammed shut and those cars were long gone, there were a few less barrels in our rack houses. Someone's pocket was getting fat, but it wasn't ours. Probably some local sheriffs, or some distant cousins, or some forward-thinking former distillery worker who had kept an extra rack house key. Anyway, a lot of that bourbon went, and it probably went to Chicago.

The Beams hunkered down during that period, did what they had to do to survive. One cousin went off to Mexico to start a distillery; making whiskey was legal there. Another went off to Montana to make "medicinal" bourbon. That's right, during Prohibition, bourbon suddenly became government-approved medicine, good for what ails you. A handful of distilleries stayed alive by getting permits to sell their whiskey to drugstores that could then turn around and sell it to people who had a prescription from a doctor. (I would love to see one of those prescriptions: *Take two tablespoons of bourbon as needed. This medicine might make you drowsy—or really happy.*) I may be wrong, but I don't think anyone made much money doing that, but every dime helped back then, I guess.

Prohibition hurt all of Kentucky and people did what they could to get by. Moonshining, supposedly named because it was made up in the hills at night when the moon was shining, became common. The 'shiners made what they could with whatever ingredients they had. The result was a whiskey of dubious quality. Some of what they made was flat-out dangerous; you could go blind drinking a bad batch, and more than a few poor souls did. Buyer beware.

Once it was made, the 'shiners poured it into Mason jars and bootlegged it out, the law not far behind. There was a famous sheriff from that time, "Big Six" Henderson, who was hell-bent on taking Prohibition seriously. He chased a lot of people around, reportedly caught a cousin or two up in the hills, shut down or broke up a lot of stills in the area. There was a fair amount of pistol waving and shotgun shooting during those years. Exciting and dangerous times. Old-timers have told me that Bardstown was a main staging area for bootleggers; they'd load up and make a run for it. There was a road not too far from the Beam house that led out of town. It was nicknamed "Alcohol Avenue," and apparently it was a main whiskey thoroughfare. Late at night, you could hear engines roaring as the cars headed off to Louisville and other big cities. The risks were high; if they got caught it was jail for sure, but the rewards—cash money in your pocket—were higher, so they drove like hell.

It's a well-known fact that NASCAR, the stock car circuit, got its start during Prohibition. Sounds strange, but it's true. The very first drivers were bootleggers. Those drivers souped up their cars, put powerful engines in them so they could outrun the tax agents, then learned to drive those hilly back roads at high speeds late at night, sometimes throwing cans of oil out their windows to make the road behind them slick. They honed their driving skills, became masters of their car, knew how to take a country road curve at 80 miles per hour, spin around 360 degrees on a dirt path, change a blowout in less than two minutes. Pretty soon those drivers began racing each other on Sunday afternoons for fun; later on they started doing it for money and another industry was born. Legendary NASCAR driver Junior Johnson was a bootlegger, although he wasn't from Kentucky.

In addition to bootlegging, there were other crimes in the Bardstown area during that time. Warehouse robberies weren't that uncommon. Transporters, or "white mule runners," would break into warehouses that still had barrels in them, siphon off the whiskey, and replace it with water. No one was the wiser. Most times the mule runners weren't that polite. They'd just pull up in a big truck, over-power the guards, tie them up, and take what they wanted. A month or two later, they'd be back for more.

Prohibition had an impact, all right. Before the law went into effect, there were 17 large distilleries operating in the Bardstown area. Kept a lot of people employed, a lot of fami-lies in groceries. But when they shut down, hard times hit and most of the distilleries went dark for good. They couldn't wait out the storm. The families that owned them—good families, friends of my family—just walked away.

We didn't, though. Somehow, Jim Beam got us through it and when Repeal came on December 5, 1933, he was ready. He was pushing 70 by then, but he still wore that suit and tie, still had a plan, still had the fire in him. Get out of my way, let me do my job. He applied for a rein-statement of his liquor-making license, then spent a year trying to get financing in order. Finally, in 1934 and with the help of his son T. Jeremiah, his brother Park, and his nephew Carl, they rebuilt that old Murphy Barber plant from scratch, bit by bit, renamed it the James B. Beam Distilling Company, and got it up and running in less than 120 days. The first post-Prohibition whiskey was sold about a year later. It was a real family effort, a high point in our history, everyone working together to preserve the leg-acy, the heritage, and even though they were crunched for time and money, they pulled it off. The Good Times, they were back.

Well, maybe not all the way back. Prohibition was like death to the bourbon distillers. As soon as the law was lifted, scotch, gin, and Canadian whiskies flooded the market. Remember, they hadn't stopped making that stuff in Canada and Scotland, so those distilleries were ready to go, they were chomping at the bit. Meanwhile, we pretty much had to start over: grind up the corn, distill it, and most important, age it. It takes time to age bourbon whiskey, years, and people weren't about to wait years. Hell, they had waited long enough for a drink. So they turned to scotch, gin, and Canadian and Irish whiskies. We were all but forgotten. Bourbon, hell, what's that again?

To make matters worse, a lot of the post-Prohibition bourbon was inferior whiskey. We and the other distillers rushed young whiskey to market or took old whiskey and added neutral spirits to it in an effort to stretch it, make it go further. The result wasn't high quality and this caused even loyal customers to look elsewhere for a cocktail.

But we kept on at it. Jim and Uncle Jere, Uncle Park, and Cousin Carl worked hard, worked their asses off, but hard work sometimes isn't enough. They needed money and thanks to Prohibition, they didn't have much. So, after I'm sure some thought and some debate and a few late nights, and a few trips to the bank and a few more trips to the accountants, and another trip to the bank, they decided to sell a big chunk of the distillery to a group of investors in Chicago, who gave them a free hand in running things. A few years later, they sold off the rest. My family had lost their independence but had gained the freedom to pursue their life's work. They got production moving again, brought what was left of our inventory to market, and probably bought other, bankrupt distilleries' inventory as well. Then they hit the road, promoting it all over the country. Billboards went up on the side of the highways, lifelong relationships with retailers and distributors were forged, ads in magazines taken out. The Beams are good at making whiskey, but we're also pretty good at selling it. In the 1950s, Colonel James B. Beam (later to be named Jim Beam Bourbon) was a national brand, and things were humming along.

Jim Beam kept running as fast as he could, but you can't outrun time and age, and pretty soon he said, "That's it," and turned the operation over to Jere. Time to head off to the front porch. In Kentucky, people don't ride off into the sunset, don't head out to pasture; they sit on the front porch. And he had one of the best front porches in Kentucky. Wide and sturdy and overlooking North Third Street, Bardstown's main drag. Jim watched the world go by from that porch for a few years, then on Christmas Eve 1947 he gave my father, Booker, his Winchester Model 12 shotgun—good for hunting quail, he said—and the next morning, Christmas Day, he died in his own home, in his own bed, 83 years old, a life lived.

I guess you could say things changed after that, and they did and they didn't. A few years before, and with Jim's blessing, a nephew, Earl, Park Beam's son, had gone to work for another distillery, and we no longer owned the business, but we still were in charge, we were still making bourbon whiskey. Uncle Jere and my cousin Carl, and later his sons, Baker and David—good old Kentucky boys you didn't mess with—did more than just preserve the legacy; they grew the business during the fifties, sixties, and seventies, gave everything they had, put their hearts and backs into it. They lived right there at the distillery, the plant a part of the family, a living and breathing thing. They took care of it, through floods, tornadoes, and lightning strikes, and it took care of them. Sales soared, and then we got bought by American Tobacco, which later became Fortune Brands, which later took us public, so we were independent again. An American company, now a global company selling more than six million cases of Jim Beam Bourbon every year, along with a lot of other bourbons and spirits.

But I'm getting way ahead of myself. In 1950, my dad, Booker, entered the picture. Big man, big ideas. (More on him later; he deserves his own chapter.) He was close to Uncle Jere, a favorite, had a knack for the business and soon enough was named Master Distiller. Booker worked for more than 50 years at our distilleries (we had two by then, one in Boston, Kentucky, and the flagship in Clermont), increasing production year after year, broadening our portfolio of brands, introducing higher-end bourbons. In short, making sure things got done right and that the foundation was solid for the next generation.

And that next generation, a seventh generation, slowly but surely came along. I'm referring to me, of course. Lucky Seven. Yours truly.

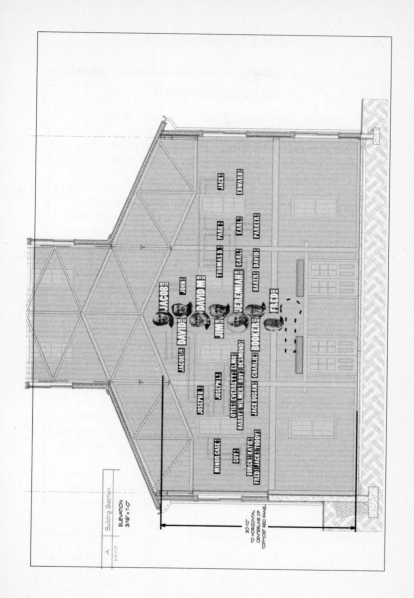

BOURBON PRIMER

Behind Every Good Bourbon There's A Beam

There are a lot of Beams in Kentucky. Always have been, probably always will be. We have a reunion every year next to the distillery, organized by my first cousin Jim Beam Noe, who is an engineer at the Clermont Plant. More than 100 people show up and we have a big time. Thumb through the Bardstown phone book and you'll see a lot more Beams. Our family tree bears out our size, and a little more research will bear out our influence in the bourbon industry. I have a long line of cousins and uncles that have worked not only at our distillery, but for competitors as well. A second cousin, Joseph, helped found Heaven Hill. Another cousin, Jack, founded the Early Times Distillery. And another Beam, Elmo, was a Master Distiller at Maker's Mark. The list goes on and on, stretching back more than 200 years. While there aren't a whole lot of direct descendants of Jim Beam, there are a whole lot of cousins. Joe Beam was one of them, for example. He was Jim's cousin, and he had seven sons and those sons were all distillers, every last one of them. All told, more than 30 descendants of Jacob Beam became distillers, whether for our company or others. It's a who's-who in whiskey and kind of flat-out amazing when you think about it.

Some families have lawyers in them, some have politicians; others have their share of writers, poets, or bankers. My family is full of distillers. Bourbon in our blood, bourbon in our bones.

JAMES B. BEAM
BARDSTOWN, KENTUCKY
December 7th 1933

Ass't Supervisor of Permits,
Bureau of Industrial Alcohol,
Louisville, Kentucky.

Dear Sir:

The undersigned, James B. Beam, President
of the James B. Beam Distilling Co., located at Clermont, Ky., herewith is enclosing application for permit to operate a distillery at Clermont, Kentucky,
said distillery to have a daily capacity of 600 bus-
hels, producing approximately 3,000 gallons of Bourbon whiskey.

James B. Beam has been engaged in the whiskey business for forty years succeeding his father D.M.
Beam in the year of 1894, since that time he has been
general manager and part owner of the Clear Spring Distilling Co., located at Bourbon, Ky., also President of
the F.G. Walker Co., located at Bardstown, Ky., and has
had full control of the two above-mentioned distilleries
up to the time of prohibition.

Now, since repeal of the 18th amendment, I am
desirous of re-entering the business and hope that your
bureau will give the application due consideration in
granting the James B. Beam Distilling Co., the permit as
requested to operate the distillery as described above.

Thanking you for your attention, I beg to remain

Yours very truly

James B. Beam

James B. Beam
for
James B. Beam Distilling Co., Inc.

Letter Asking for Permission to Operate a Distillery After Repeal

2

A KENTUCKY BOYHOOD

My first recollection of going to the distillery was when I was about seven years old. We lived in Bardstown, of course, about 15 miles from the Clermont plant, right next door to my great-grandfather's house on North Third Street. Jim Beam was long gone when I came around, but his wife, Mary (the aforementioned Maw Maw Beam), and his daughter, Mimi, lived there, so family was as close as you could get.

My dad, Booker, was committed to the plant. It was like his other son, my older brother. He spent a lot of time there, gone by 6:00 AM, back at 7:00 PM, dinner, then maybe back to the plant to fix something that broke down, or get up in the middle of the night because the night manager had gone home sick. I could have gotten jealous of the distillery, it took a lot of my dad's time and I was an only child, but instead I was curious. Wanted to know what was up over there. Wanted to be part of whatever my dad was part of. Wanted to see what the big deal was, see what was taking my father away.

So, one day, he took me over there. I think it was a Sunday, but I can't be sure. I was sitting in the back seat of the Ford Fairlane, window down, and we rounded a curve and it came into view. Smoke was coming out of the stack, I saw that first; then over some train tracks, past a guard house, and there we were. It was big and it was quiet and I smelled something sweet in the air and knew mash was cooking somewhere. I closed my eyes tight and sucked in a lungful. So far, so good, I thought.

My dad took a few minutes to show me around, then told me he'd be right back, there was something he had to check on, and disappeared into the fermenting room. I remember standing there, looking up at the rack houses, full of aging barrels of bourbon—tall, dark, mysterious buildings staring down at me. I felt there might be ghosts up there, my uncles, my great-grandfathers, my cousins, thought they might be whispering. If they were, they were probably saying, "So here's the new kid. Next in line. Good Lord, we got some work to do."

We didn't stay long that first time, but we came back again and again, and soon enough Booker took the leash off and let me run free. Kid at Christmas. I got to climb on the trucks, blow the horns, jump up in the trains when they stopped to deliver our grain, eat lunch with the other workers. My favorite thing to do, though, was fish in the hot-water pond. We had a pond that we pumped hot water into after we were done with it, and no one, especially Booker, thought there was any fish in it.

"God damn, boy, there's no fish in that hole—too damn hot!

But I believed otherwise, brought my rod with me every weekend, kept at it and one day, a Saturday, I caught a sunfish, and the next day, a bunch of bluegill. Booker couldn't understand it. "Let me look at that fish," he said. He inspected them, sniffed them, looked at me, looked at the fish, tried to figure out which one of us was lying, then walked away, mumbling "God damn" under his breath. After a while, word got out and that pond became a regular fishing hole for workers. Eventually, even Booker threw a line in. I was always proud that I "discovered" that fishing hole and regarded it as my special place. For years, I thought the ghosts in the rack houses were looking after me, keeping it stocked.

I never gave much thought to my future at the distillery when I was a boy. The plant was just a big playground to me. Booker didn't really make a point of teaching me anything at that time. Every so often, he would show me the still, or take a walk with me through the rack houses, which were dark and cool like an early spring night, and point things out, explain why we didn't heat or cool our rack houses, or how and why we stacked our barrels. Once in a while, he would stop and knock the bung out of a barrel and let me stick my nose inside it.

"Take a deep breath. Keep your eyes closed, go on," he said. And I would do as told, get a good whiff of my sweet past and future.

For the most part, though, Booker just let me roam. My older cousins were there, Baker and David, and I got to watch them work. I was impressed with what they did, how seriously they took their jobs. Baker kind of became a role model for me. He's Jim Beam's great-nephew, but he didn't have any special favors thrown his way. Even though his last name was Beam, he started out in the labor pool, raking leaves and cleaning out septic tanks. He worked his ass off for years and eventually made his way all the way up to be the distiller of the Clermont plant. I always thought he personified the family: a low-key, hardworking whiskey man. I'm glad they named a bourbon after him, and glad it was one of our best ones; hell, he deserves it.

My favorite Baker memory involves trucks. I loved the ones at the plant and lucky for me, so did Baker. He used to drive an 18-wheeler through Kentucky to pick up rye and other grains. One year on my tenth birthday, as a big surprise, Booker got me up at 4:30 and took me down to Baker's house, and there was Baker waiting in a truck. Baker kind of looked like the Marlboro Man, tall and lean with a mustache and dark hair.

"What are you staring at? Hop in," he said, and I jumped up. I spent the day hauling rye with my cousin, back and forth from Louisville, sitting in the cab, listening to country music with the window down a crack, smelling the wet Kentucky morning. As good as it gets.

When I wasn't at the distillery, I was busy being a boy in Bardstown, the Bourbon Capital of the World. Let me tell you about my hometown now; it's important, the center stage of my life. It was a small town of about 3,000 people back then, a lot of whom had whiskey roots. It wasn't exactly Mayberry, more like Mayberry on bourbon. I've been told that right after Prohibition, it was a pretty wild place. People came from Louisville and Lexington and sometimes all the way from Cincinnati to party; the world's biggest distilleries were located within a 60-mile radius, so we weren't going to run out of whiskey anytime soon. In fact, Bardstown used to be called "The Partiest Town in America." There was even a book written about it, a somewhat scandalous book, called *We'll Sing One Song*, which told out-of-school stories about Bardstown and its residents.

I'll be honest, I've never read the entire book, just parts of it. But from what I could tell, it got Bardstown right:

> . . . the tall honey locusts, the stately old houses, some in disrepair, some with tourists signs on their lawns, but

gracious, still with dignity that could not be destroyed
by years or weather;

It's a fairly lively town . . . when you get to know it.
We have as much activity per capita here as Lo'ville or
Cincinnati. You won't get bored.

That book was supposed to be fiction, but names had
been changed to protect the innocent, and everyone knew
it. My mom, Annis, said it was the talk of the town for
years and the author, Olive Carruthers, wasn't too popular after it came out. But I think she was related somehow
to William, who was married to my Aunt Mimi, so they
left her alone. Aunt Mimi ended up eventually divorcing
William, but not because of the book, though that probably didn't help things.

That was all before my time though. When I came
around, Bardstown was a pretty quiet place. There was only
noise twice a day: at noon, when the Bardstown Volunteer
Fire Department blew its siren (we called that the lunch
whistle), and when they blew it again at six (we called that
the dinner whistle). I was never was sure why they thought
that was necessary, but until this day, every time I hear a
siren, no matter where I am in the world, I get hungry.

We lived a few blocks from the downtown. Little
stores, shops. An A&P. We had two movie theaters, the
Arco and the Melody, an ice cream shop called the B&B
where I spent too much time, and a hardware store where
our local judge, Freeman Carruthers, worked. (Not sure if
he was related to the esteemed author; remember, this is

Kentucky, land of four million people and ten last names.) Judge Carruthers wasn't even a lawyer, but he was a judge, so if you had a problem, you had to go down to Grigsby Hardware and hope he wasn't too busy selling fertilizer or screwdrivers so you could plead your case. When he saw you coming, he would point a finger at you and say, "What kind of bird don't fly?" And you would say, "A jail bird," because by then, you would know the answer. He would laugh, he always thought that was funny and if you were smart, you would laugh too, hoping to curry his favor. Most times, if it was just a ticket and you promised to tell your parents what you had done, he would let you off; he wanted to get back to selling fertilizer, his true calling.

I grew up in the house I live in now, on North Third Street, which used to be called Distiller's Row, because a lot of distillers had homes on that street. The Samuels family, who started up Maker's Mark, lived two doors down, and John Schenley, another prominent distiller, lived across the street. Big old Southern-style homes, testaments to America's Native Spirit, bourbon. Bardstown was a distilling town back then. It still is to some degree, but when I was growing up, pretty much everyone either worked at or had someone in their family working at a distillery in some capacity. As I mentioned, we had a number of distilleries within an hour's drive. Being a Beam wasn't a big deal. We were just another family connected to the business. And it wasn't a glamorous business; it was honest, hard work.

Booker, my mom, Annis, and I lived next door to the Big House where my Aunt Mimi, Jim Beam's daughter, lived. The two houses used to be connected—they had been a girl's school around the turn of the century (the Bardstown Female Academy, to be exact)—but when Jim Beam bought it in 1900, he divided them up: Big House, Small House. We lived in the Small House.

Aunt Mimi, Jim Beam's daughter,* had the Big House. By then, my great-grandmother, Maw Maw Beam, was dead so Mimi had it all to herself, which was a good thing because she needed the space, she needed room. Aunt Mimi didn't like kids, but she did like Salem cigarettes, parties, bourbon cocktails, Cadillac cars, and, for some reason, me. When I was young, I would lie awake at night and hear people laughing, the piano playing, cars coming and going next door. Pretty much a constant commotion. The next day, I would get up and sneak over there and her cook, Emma, would make me breakfast. Ham, fried eggs, beaten biscuits. Eventually,

*Jim Beam had one son and two daughters: Jere, Mildred (Mimi), and Margaret, my grandmother. Margaret married Frederick Booker Noe, which is how I got my name. I should have told you that earlier, in case you wondered if I really was a Beam.

Aunt Mimi would make her way down to the kitchen, a Salem dangling from her bottom lip, face a tad puffy, eyes a little red. She would nod a silent hello, pour herself a black coffee, and plop down in a chair across the table from me.

"What are you drinking?" she asked me some mornings.

"Milk," I would say. I was six.

"Milk," she said. "Smart boy. Stick with it. Stick with it as long as you can."

In addition to me, Salem cigarettes, and parties, Aunt Mimi liked one other thing: Bourbon. Not just the whiskey now, but her Doberman Pinscher. Bourbon was big and brown and looked like he had been raised by the Devil, which was the rumor in Bardstown because he was a nasty-looking dog, growled at you if you breathed too loud. When I took him for walks, people would cross the street and avert their gaze. Bourbon always looked hungry.

Booker was never too crazy about that dog. Was suspicious of him. Thought he had too much influence in the family. The feeling was mutual. I don't think Bourbon was too crazy about Booker either. For years they kept their distance, but one Christmas, things came to a boil.

We were all driving in Aunt Mimi's Cadillac to my other Aunt Mimi's (remember, Kentucky; we're scarce on names) when Bourbon started putting his big, evil head on Aunt Mimi's shoulder. I was driving in the front with my mom while Booker, Mimi, and Bourbon were in the back.

Well, Booker didn't think that was proper. He didn't like the idea of a dog, especially a dog that was rumored to have been born and bred in Hell, nuzzling his favorite aunt on the birthday of our Savior, so he raised a polite objection.

"Get your damn head off of her!" he yelled, and yanked at Bourbon's collar.

Bourbon took offense to this. He bared his teeth and gave out one of his best and loudest growls. Now most men, when confronted by a growling Doberman Pinscher, especially a Doberman Pinscher that was sitting six inches from you, would proceed with extreme caution at this point. But my dad, Booker, was not most men. He was about six foot four, 300 pounds of Kentucky Mean, and he didn't fear anything on Planet Earth, other than maybe an empty liquor cabinet on Saturday night. He growled right back.

Things were deteriorating fast, breaking down, and when Bourbon started barking and my dad started yelling some very un–Christmas Day things in the back seat, I feared the worst. I looked in the rearview mirror, not sure who was going to bite who first. Fortunately, Aunt Mimi intervened. Unfortunately for my dad, she took Bourbon's side of the argument.

"Leave that dog alone now, Booker! Just leave him alone."

"God damnit, he started it."

"Get your hands off of him."

"Tell him to get his paws off of me!"

And so forth.

When we got to the other Aunt Mimi's house in Lebanon, everyone thought it would be best if Bourbon and Booker had some space put between them. After some discussion, it was finally decided that Bourbon would stay outside in the cold, although Aunt Mimi was lobbying hard for it to be Booker. And it was also decided that I would spend the day with him. So I ended up walking that dog around the block about 30 times that Christmas, wondering what everyone was having for dinner.

Aunt Mimi was more than all right. There was an air of wildness and excitement about her, an unpredictability. Not everyone liked being around her because she was a Beam and Beams speak their minds, but I loved her through and through and spent a lot of time over at the Big House. We had meals together, watched TV together, went into town for ice cream. After she got divorced, she took up with George Allen Barnes, who owned a produce store. George Allen Barnes would pick her up for a night on the town in his old truck that smelled like cabbage and onions, and many times Aunt Mimi would let me tag along.

"What the hell is she doing in that truck anyway?" Booker asked my mom one day at dinner. "She won't even sit in a Cadillac that's more than three years old."

"She gets in there because Fred likes that truck," my mom answered.

Booker shook his head, gave me a look. "God damn, boy, you have her tied around your little finger."

If I did, it wasn't intentional. Aunt Mimi had taken a shine to me and I to her. When George Allen Barnes showed up, she would make me a Shirley Temple and let me stand up in the back of his pickup while we cruised through the streets of Bardstown at dusk. I remember sipping on those Shirley Temples, smelling my aunt's cigarette smoke, and watching the street lights flicker on. A person's life is made up of moments; some stay with you forever, and those nights were as special as they get.

I ended up moving in with Aunt Mimi during my college years, got even closer to her. She was getting on in age and Booker asked me to come home from school and live with her for a while, she needed the help. I was happy to oblige—family is family—so I came home from Lexington, where I was going to the University of Kentucky, and helped out, did the chores, kept her company. Every night at 6 PM we'd have cocktail hour. We'd sit down in the parlor in big overstuffed chairs and have ourselves a drink and discuss the day. It was a ritual and we never missed it. It was during those evenings, before dinner, when she would tell me stories about my great-grandfather, Jim Beam. What kind of person he was like—how passionate he was about the family business, how proud he was to be a distiller and a Kentuckian. Those talks helped me appreciate the family legacy, helped me understand that I was part of something special. Aunt Mimi was proud of being a Beam, and our talks went a long way to instilling that same pride in me.

"You got to uphold the family name," she would say. "People are going to be watching you, especially in this town. Your great-grandfather, your uncles, your cousins, they all worked hard to make that name mean something, you have to remember that. When your time comes, you got to make us all proud."

I wasn't exactly sure what she meant when she said, "when your time comes," but I answered, "Yes, ma'am," every time the subject came up.

I spent a lot of time chauffeuring her about during those years. Aunt Mimi always seemed to have a new Cadillac, so I got to drive a nice set of wheels around town. Took her to the grocery store, to church, to visit her lady friends. She kept a running commentary on all things Bardstown from the back seat while I drove. It was right out of *Driving Miss Daisy*, and I enjoyed it. Aunt Mimi was an important link to my family's past; she provided me with an oral history of who we were, brought the legacy to life.

She died on her 82nd birthday. I was holding her hand when she passed. The nurses and doctors and my folks had all left the room, so we were alone. She was trying to tell me something, but couldn't and didn't. She was an important part of my life, really a friend more than an aunt. I miss her to this day.

People assume since I am a Beam, I've had to have led a pretty wild life. That's a pretty big assumption when you think about it. Just because we're a whiskey-making family doesn't mean we sit around all day and drink, hoot and holler, and shoot pistols off in the air or something. Besides, as I've mentioned, we're a big family and there's a lot of Beams. Some of us are wild, and some of us are flat-out boring. (I tend to avoid the boring ones.) That said, I admit, growing up I probably fell into the first camp, though I didn't shoot many pistols off. At least not until after college. (More on that later. . . .)

While I didn't commit any major, Class A felonies, I was no angel when I was young. I went to St. Joseph Parochial School in Bardstown, where I said a lot of prayers and wrote "I will not talk in class" a lot more. Saying I was an average student, something I aspired to be, would have been a major compliment. The nuns were hard on all of us, but especially me. Early on, I was singled out, had a target on my back: St. Joe's Most Wanted.

A nun named Sister Dorothy had it in for me the most. She was tough, part football coach, part Marine drill sergeant, part Bourbon the dog. I'm pretty sure she spent her nights on her knees praying for divine guidance on how to make my life miserable. And, for the most part, her prayers were answered. She made my life hell.

When she wasn't trying to save my soul by making me hold textbooks out with outstretched arms for hours at a time, or cuffing me on the back of head with the same hand she used to bless herself, she tried to get my "mind right" with something called the "the new math." The new math was an evil invention, designed to confuse and terrorize dedicated non-academics like myself. But Sister Dorothy was committed to it and attacked all those who resisted, like she was part of the Inquisition. Despite her efforts and determination, the new math wasn't taking with me, so Booker, he got involved. Every night we would sit at our round kitchen table and do homework, and every night I prayed a tornado, or an asteroid, or a tidal wave would make a direct hit on our house so I wouldn't have to sit through the tutorials. Booker was a stern and determined tutor, thought he could teach me what scores of nuns couldn't.

He also didn't think much of the new math; it was a mystery to him, an unnecessary process.

"What the hell do we need new math for? Why are they teaching you this?"

I shrugged. He was asking *absolutely* the wrong person this question.

"God damnit. The old math works fine, don't you think?"

Old math, new math. To be honest, I didn't really have much of a preference. "Yes, sir," I said.

"Damn right. Go sharpen your pencil, we got some work to do."

So he stuck with the old math, and that caused some problems back at Mission Control, St. Joe's. It all came to a head one day. Sister Dorothy flunked me on a big test, even though I had the right answers. She said I hadn't followed the proper process. When he saw my grade, Booker took umbrage. He stared long and hard at the test, his jaw clenched. "Let's go pay a visit to this nun," he finally said.

We went to school the next day and had an audience with Sister Dorothy. She sat behind her desk while Booker stood, towering over her. I kind of stood behind him in the event Sister Dorothy threw something, which she was not above doing.

"I assume you're here to discuss Freddie's failure on the last test."

"He didn't fail. He had all the right answers." For proof, Booker held up my test and politely shoved it front of Sister Dorothy's pious face. She took the test and put it down on her desk without so much as a glance.

"He didn't follow the new process."

"But he has all the right answers," Booker said.

"He didn't come to them in the correct fashion."

"But a right answer is a right answer."

Sister Dorothy was having none of it. She folded her arms across her chest, stuck out her chin. This was her attack pose. Rumor had it that she had magical powers and was capable of transforming herself into a wolf and eating people when confronted. I now moved directly behind Booker. By the time she finished eating my dad, I would be long gone, I thought. Booker would be a big meal.

"He needs to follow the new math," I heard her say.

Booker stared down at her, growled, grumbled, shuffled his feet, grumbled some more, suppressed a "God damn."

He wasn't used to not getting his way. Sister Dorothy didn't transform herself into a wolf, but she didn't budge either. She had the Lord and the religion of the new math firmly behind her, and Booker knew it. He had met his match.

"Get your coat," he told me, his eyes still on Sister Dorothy.

The next day at breakfast, Booker asked me if I wanted to go to military school in Tennessee. I asked if they had nuns there and when he said no, I said yes.

I was twelve years old when I headed off to Castle Heights Military Academy in Lebanon, Tennessee, about 150 miles southeast of Bardstown. I had been there before, but not for school, just for summer camps, and I went with my best friend, John Walters. So despite my age—I was one of the youngest boys there—I wasn't nervous or scared. I was ready for an adventure and I got it.

Castle Heights wasn't exactly West Point, but it wasn't exactly *Fast Times at Ridgemont High*, either. They took the whole military part of military school pretty seriously, so it was strict. Some of the boys went there because of the athletics—we had good football teams—but most of them went there because their parents had shipped them off. They were boys like me, "high-spirited characters" who needed to be brought down a notch or two. Or three.

We had to get up at 6:30 and put on uniforms and march in formation to breakfast, and there was inspection every Friday where some officer gave your room the white-glove treatment while you stood at attention, sucked in your gut, and prayed they didn't check under your bed. A favorite expression of the Academy was "Prior Preparation Prevents Piss Poor Performance," so we were always running around preparing for something. The Vietnam War was going on, and if the Viet Cong decided to invade Lebanon, Tennessee, well, we were ready.

Since discipline and following orders weren't exactly my strong suit, I surprisingly took to it all pretty well. I marched, I cleaned, I more-or-less studied (emphasis on the less), and I played football. And I was almost killed.

The almost-killed part happened soon after I got there. I was sitting on the steps of the Administration Building, shooting the breeze with my fellow inmates—I mean cadets—minding my own on a cloudless, windless day, counting my blessings to be away from Sister Dorothy, when out of nowhere, a huge tree branch fell on me. This wasn't a twig now, this was a *limb*. At the very last second, I jumped out of the way, but it got part of me anyway, laid me up pretty good. I was knocked cold. If I hadn't jumped when I did, I surely would have been killed. I remember lying in the hospital bed, pondering life and death, wondering why a tree would decide to fall on me, single me out, on a perfect day. Then I started wondering about Sister Dorothy, wondered if she was behind this. She had powers. You can run but you cannot hide. To this day, I still think she had something to do with my brush with death.

My parents visited me a lot, my mom missed me, so every few weekends, there they were. My mom and I were close. Booker was a handful, and she and I would team up to weather his moods together. She was the complete opposite of Booker; quiet, religious, patient. We looked out for each other. It wasn't her idea to send me away, it was Booker's decision, but, as I said, I was ready for the change, and while I missed her, I didn't really miss home.

When they came down to the Academy, Booker brought whiskey for all the teachers, cases of bourbon. He would pass them out from the back of his trunk with a smile and a pat on the back. The faculty loved him. He was like a bourbon Santa Claus, except he came twice a month and he didn't care if you were naughty or nice, just that you didn't flunk his son out. Looking back on it, that's probably why I lasted six years there.

I eventually fell in with older boys; they met Booker, found out who I was related to, put two and two together, and became my best friends. I ran pretty fast and hard with them. There was a creek in back of campus and late at night, we'd slip out our windows, avoid Shorty, the night watchman, and meet up and party, have a big time.

There were a set of keys at the Academy, sacred keys that unlocked every door in the place. They had been stolen years before from a teacher by some seniors, and each year these keys were passed down to the next class. Never in the history of the Academy did anyone other than a senior get to have those keys. But in my sophomore year, they were presented to me. It was a big honor, a solemn responsibility.

I probably got those keys because I was as wild as most of the seniors. I also got them, I suppose, because of my family tree. While I was hardly a celebrity, I know being a Beam made me stand out. That was the first time I felt that, felt a little different. Being a Beam in Bardstown didn't mean much, we were all Beams pretty much, but away from home, for better or worse, it drew attention.

That family tree helped me get those keys and those keys meant freedom, access. My friends and I took full advantage, unlocking classroom doors late at night, smoking cigarettes and purposely leaving the butts on the teacher's desk, finding the answers to tests, raiding the kitchen. When I finally graduated, I handed the keys over to another boy, told him to treat them with respect. Those keys helped get me through the Academy. And I needed all the help I could get.

Despite the change from St. Joe's, I wasn't motivated, knew I wasn't going to make the military a career. I just wanted to hang with my buds, party, do the minimum to get by in the classroom, wait for the weekend. I was in and out of trouble, collected a boxful of demerits and demotions. I knew I was frustrating my family, letting them down, but I was a kid, something of a rebel, and that was the way it was.

Near graduation, the woman at the post office, a tiny little thing, made an interesting observation about me. She said, "You're in and out of trouble so much that you remind me of another boy we had here not too long ago. Greg."

I shrugged, picked up my mail, turned to leave. I wasn't all that interested in some Greg.

"Yes, sir, Greg Allman, he was a piece of work. Wonder what ever happened to him? Probably no good."

To sum it up, my military career wasn't exactly stellar. I went into Castle Heights Military Academy a private and six years later, left Castle Heights Military Academy* a private, which, I was told, was *highly* unusual.

After I graduated, Booker told me I could go to any college I wanted, as long as I could get in. I pondered this decision for a while. Since I never had given college much thought, I decided I better do some research to help me find the right academic institution that fit my selective criteria for higher education. I picked up *Playboy* magazine, saw a list of Best Party Schools in America, saw that Western Kentucky University over in Bowling Green was rated number two in the nation, and closed the magazine.

My exhaustive research was concluded.

*If you're interested in ever visiting the Castle Heights Military Academy or maybe sending your son there in hopes of straightening him out, don't bother. It no longer exists. The campus is now the headquarters of the Cracker Barrel Corporation, which I find funny and a little ironic; I really like the Cracker Barrel.

BOURBON PRIMER

I think it would only be right that I spend a little time talking about how bourbon is made. I'm making an assumption, since you're reading this book, that you have an interest in the process. I'll try to keep this as simple as possible. As you no doubt have surmised by now, I have a strong aversion to textbooks and people posing as teachers.

Before I go any further, I want to talk about how bourbon got called bourbon. As I mentioned earlier, bourbon got its name from the county in Kentucky where it came from—Bourbon County, which was named after the French royal family for all of their help during the Revolutionary War. So the county is kind of a big thank-you note to France. (Actually, now that I think about it, a lot of Kentucky towns and cities are named after the French: Louisville, Versailles, Fayette. We've even got a Paris. If nothing else, we Kentuckians are *appreciative*.)

Originally, Bourbon County comprised about one-third of the state. When they started making whiskey, it was just called whiskey but that eventually changed. Whiskey from Bourbon County eventually became Bourbon Whiskey. According to some research, the first time that name appeared in print was about 1820, in a local newspaper ad. (*Kentucky Bourbon: The Early Years of Whiskeymaking*, by Henry. G. Crowgey, page 121, if you don't believe me.) Over time, Bourbon County shrank; they kept carving other counties out of it, and now it's relatively small in size. Ironically enough, for years it was dry, too. Go figure.

So now that we have the name figured out, let's move on to what bourbon is: it's a whiskey. Now, I'll tell you what whiskey is, since that's the natural next question: it's a spirit that's made from a grain like corn, rye, wheat, or barley. Bourbon is a whiskey because it's mostly made up of corn and rye (though some have wheat). To be able to call a whiskey a bourbon, it has to be made up of at least 51 percent corn, and it has to be aged at least two years inside charred, new oak barrels that can only be used once. If we reuse a barrel, whatever is inside it can't be called bourbon.

All bourbon is whiskey, but not all whiskey is bourbon. Other whiskies include scotch (main ingredient, malted barley), Canadian (rye), and Irish (malted barley). Those are all good whiskies, but they're not bourbon. Bourbon is the best, at least in my not-so-impartial opinion.

The process starts with corn. We use field corn mostly from Kentucky, Indiana, and Illinois. We grind it up when we get it, and we add other small grains like rye and malted barley, and then we cook it with water.

I have to make a special mention of the water here, because it is special. The water Kentucky distillers use is ideal for whiskey making. A lot of it is spring water that's naturally filtered through a limestone shelf that runs through the region. The result is water that is free of iron and rich in minerals—as sweet as water comes.

So we mix the ground-up grains with this sweet, pure water and the result is a kind of mash. We cook that up, which converts the starch in the grain to sugar. Next, we add the yeast. Each distillery has its own special yeast and we keep a close eye on ours; it's not something we share because each yeast culture is a little different, and this difference has an effect on the final taste. Also, using the same yeast culture ensures consistency in the whiskey. We don't want whiskey that tastes different from barrel to barrel.

(*continued*)

(*continued*)

Our yeast has been in the family for years. As I mentioned, Jim Beam used to cart it home with him because he was afraid the distillery would burn down or there would be a flood or earthquake or some other calamity. He was a little obsessed with his yeast.

Anyway, once the yeast is added, fermentation starts. This means sugars from the grains are broken down. At this point we have distiller's beer—a nice, sweet, soupy mixture that has a little alcohol in it. We then take that mixture and distill it, heating it on up with steam until the alcohol turns into a vapor. These vapors are cooled and condensed (turned back into liquid) and then distilled a second time. This second distillation purifies the alcohol and increases its strength. The result is a clear liquid that looks like water. We call that liquid "white dog," because if you drink too much of it, it will bite your ass like a dog.

After we've made enough of the white dog, we put it in those oak barrels that have been charred or burned on the inside and load them into our rack houses. Time and the seasons take over from there. Our rack houses don't have heat or air conditioning, so we're dependent on the weather to make things right. During the hot, humid summers, the whiskey flows into the charred wood, and during the cold winters, it contracts, flowing out. As I mentioned before, the charring creates a carmelized layer of sugar, known as "the red line." As the white dog moves in and out of the wood, it passes through that red line, picking up color and flavor along the way.

We have about 60 rack houses located throughout central Kentucky, and they house about 20,000 53-gallon barrels each, though we now have a few that store 50,000 barrels. While the rack houses are sturdy and durable and can handle most of what the weather can throw at them, they can still fall victim to severe storms. A few years back, lightning hit a rack house from another distillery and scattered barrels every which way. It was national news. Some whiskey even ended up in the Kentucky River, and the EPA had to come out to test the water to make sure it wasn't too high proof. That's the exception, though. Mostly, rack houses are built to last, and they have.

Anyway, once the whiskey has spent time getting to know the inside of a barrel, we "dump" various barrels into a vat to marry the bourbon together. For the most part, we take a vertical cross section of barrels* from our nine-story rack house. A bunch from the first floor, where it's cooler and the proof isn't as high, then more from the second, and so on, all the way up to the ninth floor where it's hot (it can get more than 100 degrees easy up there in the summer) The ninth-floor bourbon is pretty high proof, since a lot of the water has evaporated.

Once we get it all together, we cut some of it down with water to lower the proof, then bottle, ship, sell it. All in all, a pretty good system and a pretty special whiskey.

I'm not the only one who thinks so. On January 7, 1964, the U.S. Congress, under Lyndon. B. Johnson (we always say the "B" stands for "bourbon"), passed a resolution declaring that bourbon was "America's Native Spirit." The resolution declared that "whiskey is a distinctive product

---

*Most of our whiskey is taken from a vertical cross section, but Booker's is taken from the fifth floor, a horizontal cut. Also, our single-barrel Knob Creek comes from just that—single barrels. It's a great whiskey.

(*continued*)

(*continued*)

of the United States and is unlike other types of alcoholic beverages." This means that bourbon can only be made in America.

Who says Congress never accomplishes anything?

In summary, here's a handy pocket guide to what makes a whiskey a bourbon. It must:

- Be made up of at least 51 percent corn
- Come off the second distillation no more than 160 proof (80 percent alcohol; proof is always twice the alcohol content)
- Be aged to no more than 125 proof in new, charred, white oak barrels for a minimum of two years to be called straight bourbon
- Have no coloring or flavoring added to it
- Bottled at a minimum of 80 proof
- Be made in America (For the record, it can be made in states other than Kentucky, but for the most part it's not. About 90 percent of the world's bourbon is made in Kentucky. I don't know where the other 5 or 10 percent comes from, but I tell you what: I wouldn't drink it.)

A Little Tidbit

Back in the old days, bourbon was more than just a drink to take the edge off a hard day of plowing or fighting off bears. It was also currency; it was sold and bartered for food, livestock, clothing, and even land. Legend has it that Abraham Lincoln's father, Tom, sold the family farm in Kentucky for $20 and 10 barrels of whiskey before moving on to Indiana, then Illinois. Unfortunately, housing prices haven't changed that much in Kentucky.

3

BOOKER: YES, SIR.

I think it might make sense for me to take break from talking about myself, switch gears, and talk about my dad, Booker. I've already given you a glimpse of him, but as I said, he deserves his own chapter. He loomed large in my life, was a significant presence. He also had a big impact on the bourbon industry, and played a role in shaping it into what it is today.

Like a lot of fathers and sons, Booker and I had our moments. Good, bad, bad, good. I know I frustrated him at times: my partying, my decisions, my lack of direction. Hell, I drove him plain nuts at times. But in the end, we turned out all right together, stuck by each other. That's the whole point of family, isn't it? You tough it out, weather the storms, and leave on a high note.

I guess you could say that my dad was a character, an American original. Did what he wanted, said what he wanted, ate and drank what he wanted. He was Kentucky, bourbon, and Beam, all blended together: uncut, unfiltered, and high, high proof.

He was born on December 7 (which would eventually become a day of infamy for another reason) in 1929, just as the stock market was collapsing, so at first people called him Hard Times. It was a nickname that didn't really stick since his real name, Booker, was pretty catchy in its own right. (For the record, and in case you're keeping score, his Christian name was Frederick Booker Noe, II, which, minus the "II" part, was his father's name, which also happens to be my name and, wouldn't you know it, my son's name. Not sure what we would do if we'd had any girls.)

Booker was born in nearby Springfield, Kentucky, but soon moved over to Bardstown to go to boarding school. By all accounts, he had a childhood somewhat similar to mine. He played football in high school, then spent about a semester at the University of Kentucky, after receiving a scholarship to play for a coach named Bear Bryant, before dropping out. This disappointed Uncle Jere to no end. Booker was his boy; Uncle Jere loved him, loved UK, and loved football, so he took the news hard. So Booker, embarrassed and ashamed, hit the road, hitchhiking across the country. He was gone for months; no one knew where he was and it was the talk and mystery of Springfield. Just up and vanished. He eventually surfaced in New Mexico, broke and hungry and about to enlist in the Air Force because they promised to feed him, when my family got wind of his whereabouts and wired him some money to come home, which he did. Soon after, he went to work at the Clermont plant, where Uncle Jere and Cousin Carl trained him. I sometimes wonder how different my life would have been if he had gone Air Force. Hell, I'd probably be the world's oldest private right now.

He eventually met up with my mom, Annis, a slight, quiet woman who quickly became his better half. She was a medical technologist, was good at her job, and put in some long hours at the hospital. My mom is tiny and Booker was a grizzly bear, but they lasted close to 50 years. My mom could tell you stories about Booker, keep you up until midnight laughing, but she won't, so I will.

I think one of them, a short one, sums up his approach to life. It involves the old Ford Fairlane that he brought me home from the hospital in. He drove that car forever, piled the miles on it, drove it so hard that eventually you could see the road underneath the floor rushing by. Literally wore it out. Then one day, on the way back from the distillery, that car stopped on him like a dying horse. Couldn't go another mile. So Booker got out, pushed it off into a field, grabbed his lunch pail, and hitchhiked home. That car stayed in that field for years. I used to see it from the road when we drove by in our new car, weeds growing out of the windows, a testament to my childhood.

Although he became something of a celebrity later on in life, at least in our industry, he was, at heart, a working man. As I've already mentioned, he put in long hours at the distillery. There was nothing glamorous about what he did, and he pretty much did everything. Oversaw production, oversaw maintenance of the plants, oversaw the people who worked there. It was a job and it was his life. He never complained, not once.

As I mentioned before, he was a big man, well over six feet, and he had a low, gravelly voice that you could hear a mile away, like thunder on a prairie rolling your way. When he was mad at you, you knew it, and when you did good, you knew it. He was a Beam, straight up, no bullshit.

He started at the company in 1950 and put in long hours down there, first at Clermont, then later at the Boston, Kentucky, plant.* He did just about everything. Built this, fixed that. He could be a tough boss and wasn't above settling a labor dispute out back behind the dry house, though he didn't do that very often because most men were afraid of him.

*In 2005, the Boston plant was renamed the Booker Noe Plant in his honor.

Life at the distillery was hard and it could take a toll. After a particularly long day, he would come home, grab up a bottle, and pour himself a tall one, then go over to the kitchen sink and run the tap water cold. Then he'd swing that glass back and forth underneath the faucet, fill the rest of the glass with water and drink the whole thing down in three big gulps. (This was before bottled water, mind you.) I knew that the bigger the glass, the longer the day had been.

When he wasn't at the distillery, he fished and sometimes hunted. I remember shooting the Model 12 shotgun with him at the distillery when I was about four. Thing knocked me back on my ass, sent me flying. Booker had a big laugh over that. Every so often in the fall, we would head down to the plant to shoot pigeons that lived in the rack houses. They got inside through broken windows and nested up in the rafters, making a mess. So Booker asked some workers to go up there and make some noise to flush them, and when they flew out, Booker would pick them off with the shotgun, one by one, that old gun cracking in the evening, the sound echoing off the nearby hills.

He wasn't all outdoorsman. He liked to putter around in the kitchen, driving my mom nuts, while he worked on some concoction, some recipe for something. He fancied himself a cook and he usually made a mess of things. My mom, she was the real cook.

Booker spent years trying to perfect something called Salt-Risen Bread and Beaten Biscuits. His grandmother used to make them for him when he was a boy, and Booker spent hours trying to recreate the memories and magic. He'd camp out in the kitchen for hours, his face white with flour, sweat on his forehead, as he created. In the end, despite all his efforts and dozens of recipes, and despite the fact that I always thought they tasted pretty good, he would be disappointed in the final product and go off to sulk in the backyard, sit down and stare up at the sky, probably trying to ask his dead grandma for the divine recipe. A few days later though, he'd be back at it. He was determined, a perfectionist with everything that he did.

But he did have his areas of expertise when it came to food. He had a smokehouse in his backyard, built by Jim Beam, and he cured and smoked hams there. By the time we were living in the Big House, you weren't supposed to have a smokehouse in Bardstown; it was against the law. But our smokehouse was grandfathered in; it had been built so long ago, it was something of a local landmark and it still is.

Now, next to bourbon, smoked hams were Booker's specialty. He'd get the fresh meat, rub them down with salt, then lay them on an incline for a few weeks, until all the natural juices were drained off. Next, he'd hang them up in the smokehouse—a small, brick cylinder building in the backyard—and smoke them for a few days, using green hickory. Then he'd leave the hams alone for a long time, let them hang for two summers, until they were ready to eat. Those hams, when they were good to go, were the talk of Bardstown. When Booker cut them down it was an event; people would line up for a taste. And if you were lucky, you would get one on your doorstep at Christmas.

He loved those hams so much he would travel with them. He usually had one in the trunk of his car. "Just in case," he would say. A "just in case" happened once when he was up in Chicago visiting the corporate headquarters. He was having lunch with some Beam executives at a fancy restaurant and ordered the ham. Bad move for him. Worse move for the restaurant. The ham was poor and he did not hide his displeasure.

"This is inferior," he said to Jim, the public relations guy who always traveled with Booker. (Jim was personally assigned to Booker since Booker was always on the verge of creating an international incident every time he left Bardstown.) "Go out to the car. I have a ham in the trunk. Go bring it in here."

When Jim seemed hesitant—in Chicago you usually don't bring food *into* a restaurant—Booker began to get agitated. "Go get the damn ham," he said, throwing Jim the keys. "It's underneath my suitcase."

When Jim came back a few minutes later holding a three-pound ham in front of him like it was a newborn infant, the manager of the restaurant expressed some concern and intervened.

"Excuse me, sir, you can't bring that in here."

"Tell him that," Jim said, nodding at Booker.

The manager looked at Booker, who was wearing a big cowboy hat, and quickly recognized that he was in the presence of a Higher Ham God. He let Jim proceed and followed him to the table.

"Go get your cook," Booker said to the manager. "He needs an education in ham."

A moment later, a confused and pretty scared chef was sitting at the table watching as Booker cut him off a hunk of ham with his pocketknife. By now, every eye in the restaurant was watching the proceedings.

"Eat this," Booker said, as he handed the hunk to the chef.

The chef chewed, swallowed. "Pretty good," he said.

Booker stared right at him.

"Delicious. Wonderful," the chef said.

"Damn right it's delicious." He looked around the restaurant. "Anyone else wants some? Pull up a chair." Legend has it, he fed half the restaurant.

In addition to ham, Booker liked fish. He liked to catch it, and he liked to eat it. I fished with him a lot, starting out in the distillery, fishing the small ponds together, then later on branching out to lakes and rivers in Arkansas and Kansas, then Canada, Alaska, and the Gulf of Mexico, where he once accidentally caught a 400-pound shark that he had to shoot with a gun. It was quality time together, and next to walking inside the quiet rack houses, fishing was probably where he was most happy and content.

Later on in life, when traveling got to be a bit of a chore for him, he built himself a pond in our backyard and

stocked it with fish. The pond was really a glorified swimming pool, pretty unsightly, and it was stuffed with catfish,
bass, and bluegill. When Booker was hungry, he would go
out and try to catch something to eat. Despite the fact that
there were dozens of fish in there, sometimes Booker didn't
get a nibble, so he would stand there and quietly talk to the
fish, encourage them to take the bait, before giving up and
going back inside to make himself a ham sandwich.

Booker also liked to party. For a big man, he was a
deft dancer and he would take my mother to the Fish &
Game Club on Saturday night and cut the rug for hours,
a favorite of the ladies. His parties in Bardstown were
legendary, especially his Kentucky Derby bash. Half the
town would show up, whether they were invited or not.
Booker would hire a band and "blow into a jug" along with
the music. (He loved blowing into that jug, treated it like
it was a Stradivarius.) He also took bets, mixed up some
juleps, and cut up some ham and put it on the beaten biscuits. It was a big time.

We held this annual party with one of the family's best
friends, the Dicks. Donald Dick had been Booker's best friend
and when he passed, his wife, Toogie, spent a lot of time
with us, taking vacations, hosting dinners. She was more
or less family. Anyway, one year, my mother and Toogie
decided to send out invitations to the big party, got them
all ready to go. Booker came home from the distillery,
picked one up, scrutinized it, shook his head, then handed
it back to my mom.

"So no men are invited to the party?" he asked.

My mom was confused. "What are you talking about?"

"No men allowed?"

"What are you saying?"

He handed my mom the invitation. "Read what that says."

"What?"

"Read what you wrote. Out loud." (It's probably important to remind you here that our last name is pronounced "no.")

My mom squinted at the invitation. "'You are invited to a Noe-Dick Party.'"

"'A Noe-Dick Party,'" Toogie innocently repeated.

Booker looked at them. At first nothing registered with the women, then all of a sudden everything did.

"Oh my Lord!" said Toogie and my mom.

"Throw those things out, Annis," said Booker.

"I'll do it right now."

"Let's just call people instead," Toogie said.

"That's a good idea," my mom said.

Another memorable party involved the Blue Knights. This one didn't have any written invitations either.

The Blue Knights were a club of policemen who rode motorcycles for a hobby. Somehow Booker got hooked up with them, and went over to see them at their annual get-together in Sheperdsville to say hello, have few drinks. (Knowing Booker, he probably thought you can never have enough friends who are policemen.) So, he goes over there on Saturday night, and one thing leads to another and suddenly he's everyone's best friend and suddenly he's inviting everyone over to our house the next day for lunch.

Fast forward to breakfast the next morning. Booker, buttering up his pancakes, casually mentions to my mom that he invited some people over for lunch.

"Well, how many?"

Booker shrugs, reaches for the syrup. "Well, I never got an official count. I'd say three, four hundred."

My mom dropped her coffee cup. "Three, four *hundred*?"

"About that," Booker said chewing. "Like I said, never got an exact count, but I think that's the ballpark."

Sure enough, a few hours later, there were about 300 motorcycles on our front lawn and parked up and down the side streets. The town was overwhelmed.

We had to run out and buy every piece of meat in Bardstown. Just about cleaned out the two grocery stores. Finally they said they wouldn't sell us anymore, wouldn't be fair to the other residents, so we had to go to another town.

I remember Booker surveying the scene, his backyard full of partying policemen, sipping bourbon, eating beaten biscuits and ham, listening to a local band he had hired. "God damn," he said, "I bet I'll never get another speeding ticket as long as I live."

When he wasn't hunting and fishing and dancing and drinking, Booker made bourbon. He was good at it too, a craftsman. Took his work seriously. Under his watch, production increased; he was particularly good at what we called producing yield. He and Cousin Carl were competitive on this subject. Carl didn't like the fact that Booker, who was younger, could get more whiskey out of a bushel of grain than he could. (How much bourbon a bushel of grain would yield used to be a source of pride back then.) This quest for high yields produced some tension between them, which was only natural—show me one family business that doesn't have any tension—but they got over it. In the end, all that mattered was making good bourbon.

After a few years at the big Clermont plant, Booker started up another distillery in nearby Boston, Kentucky. It's pretty remote out there, not many visitors, off the beaten path. No one came to visit and this suited Booker just fine. Peace and quiet. Time to create. No tourists coming down to walk around like they did at Clermont. No executives from the home office stopping in to chat. This soon became his laboratory, and he began to tinker with some whiskey with good results. In time, he shared those results with friends and family and word spread. Booker was on to something. This was around 1986–87, the Big Eighties, stock market up, business booming. People were enjoying life, looking to spend some money on finer things. Eventually, the head of sales, Mike Donohoe, up in the home office in Deerfield, Illinois, got wind that Booker was on to something and called him to inquire.

"What are you making down there?" Mike said.

"Who told you I was making anything?"

"Booker, what are you drinking down there?"

"Ain't drinking nothing. Who's got time to drink? Working my ass off."

"Booker, heard you're making something special."

"God damnit," Booker said, and the secret was out.

He had wanted it all for himself: bourbon, uncut, unfiltered, taken from the center cut of the rack house, the fifth floor, where the humidity and temperature combine in perfect proportion to produce the perfect bourbon. Aged six to eight years, and bottled at barrel strength, around 125 proof. Bourbon the way it used to be, the way it was meant to be. Bourbon made in limited amounts. It changed a lot of things, not just at Beam but within the industry. Soon we were selling Booker's (he liked it so much, he named this special bourbon after himself), and a few years later we were selling Knob Creek, Basil Hayden's, and Baker's, named after my cousin. Small Batch Bourbons: higher proof, extra aged. Limited quantities, made in small batches. All top-shelf, back-of-the-bar stuff. He helped create a category—ultra-premium bourbons— and kick-started things, not just with us, but with the entire industry. In short, he helped lead a full-fledged renaissance. Bourbon wasn't your grandfather's drink anymore; you didn't have to chase it with a beer. It was right up there with single-malt scotch, connoisseur worthy. Not cheap, but worth every penny.

The Small Batch Bourbons, they put Booker on the map. Suddenly he was the talk of the whiskey world. Reporters from the *New York Times* and *Esquire* and CBS News and *GQ* wanted to come down and visit with the man with the strange name, Jim Beam's grandson.

Suddenly consumers wanted to meet this old Kentucky boy; suddenly Booker was flying all over the world, traveling, taking up two seats in coach, then later first class, spreading the word. Booker spoke in front of hundreds of people, leading Small Batch tastings in Australia, Germany, Japan, and Mexico, with people lining up for his autograph. Suddenly Booker was saying what he wanted to say in front of hundreds of people, keeping the PR team scrambling, clarifying, apologizing. Suddenly he wasn't at the distillery anymore; he was gone, that part of his life done forever.

Well, almost done forever. Despite his schedule, he kept a close eye on the process, the quality. Made sure nothing slipped while he was off in Paris, wolfing down foie gras. When he was at home, the distillery would send over samples of Booker's bourbon, and we would sit at the kitchen table and sip the whiskey, trying to decide if it was ready to be bottled or needed more time in the barrel. Many times, I would sit there with him, along with a few trusted friends, like Jerry Dalton, who lived behind us and who would later become our Master Distiller. We would sit, sip, sniff, sip, and then Booker would ask whoever was there what they thought. We would all vote, but we knew it didn't matter, because Booker had the only vote that counted.

Back on the road, my mom, and sometimes Toogie and Booker's friend Jack Kelley, who was also his lawyer, traveled with him. Sometimes I tagged along. The Booker Express. The Kentucky Mafia. For a long time, he loved it;

Booker was at home being in the center of things, being the ringmaster—step right up—but after 10 years, he eventually grew tired of the travel and the commotion. Enough's enough. He was over 70 and wanted to fish, wanted to make some more beaten biscuits. In other words, it was time to sit on the front porch, time to pass the baton. By then, I was approaching 50 years old and was kneeling in the on-deck circle, bat in hand, ready for action.

Also around that time, Booker started to get sick.

It started with a shortness of breath, which led to one thing and then another, then later a diagnosis of diabetes. This was the beginning of the end of the man I knew. Even Booker wasn't a match for that. Dialysis three times a week in Louisville, hooked up to a machine for hours at a time. No more hunting, no more fishing. No more dancing, no more parties. No more walking inside the cool, dark rack houses, smelling the sweet whiskey air, like his grandfather did, and his dad before that. Just hooked up and playing out the string. Waiting for whatever came next.

I took him back and forth to the hospital during those times, and it was during those drives together that we finally made our peace. Ever since he took me home in that Ford Fairlane, Booker had had high hopes for me, high standards, standards I had at times failed to meet, standards I thought that were impossible to meet. (The only answer he ever wanted to hear from me was "Yes, sir.")

I had been a wild kid; had long hair, lived to party, stay out all night, didn't care about a whole lot besides getting to Saturday night. The last year or so, though, as I took over his role as spokesperson and ambassador of the company (more on that later), I could tell he was proud of me. I don't think he ever thought I could do it, and when I did, I suspect I surprised him. So we were already on a pretty good path when he got sick, but the diabetes brought us even closer together. Those trips back and forth to Louisville, those afternoons waiting for this treatment to end, we did a lot of talking. Closure, I guess that's what they call it. A lot of fathers and sons don't ever get it, so I guess we were lucky we did.

We talked about the business, talked about my son Freddie, even talked a little bit about life and death. He opened up about things, said he knew he had been hard on me. Told me he was proud of me. I had waited a long time to hear those words and they meant a lot.

After a while, his conditioned worsened and the doctor said they would have to amputate his foot. I was there when the doctor told Booker. He fell quiet and did some thinking.

"Say I don't go through with it. What would happen?" Booker asked.

"I would strongly advise that you do. This is very serious. It would be life threatening."

Booker got quiet again. "And say I stop with the treatment, how long would I live?"

"Stop the dialysis? Not long, a few weeks at most."

Booker got to thinking again, thought long and hard, looked down at the floor and considered things. Then he pushed himself up out of his chair. "Why don't you go on and cancel my treatment from now on."

"Booker!"

"I'm done. Going home. You been a good doctor. Did the best you could. Fred, get my hat."

We didn't say much on the drive back to Bardstown. My head was swimming, didn't know what to say. Hard to talk about the weather or UK basketball in that situation. Finally, Booker asked for my opinion.

"What do you think about what I'm doing?"

I was quiet, then softly said, "It's your call. But you may want to think on it."

"I have been thinking about it." He went quiet and he looked out the window. We were getting off the expressway and pretty soon we would be driving right by the distillery.

"You know," he said, "life's not about quantity, it's about quality. I've lived a quality life, that's all that matters. Don't care how long I live, never have. It's always been *how* I live."

"Yes, sir."

"And you don't have to call me 'sir' anymore, god damnit."

"Yes, sir," I said again, and then we laughed, which probably kept me from crying.

When we got back home, Booker got busy dying. Word got out and soon everyone in three states was stopping by to say goodbye, share one more story, have one more drink, though Booker could only take a sip. Our house was never empty. Booker wanted to be cremated and have his remains put in a specially designed wooden box, along with his lucky hat and the very first bottle of Booker's ever produced. Two local men, friends of Booker's, designed the box, and Booker made them come over to the house and show it to him. I guess he wanted to make sure it was perfect since he would be spending eternity in it. The men were crying real tears when they showed up and Booker, propped up in bed, offered them a drink. "Relax, boys, you've done a good job." Jack Kelley, his best friend, said it best: "Leave it to Booker to be alive at his own wake."

Three weeks after he got home, he died in his bed, the same bed his grandfather Jim Beam died in, another life lived. Half of Kentucky came to his funeral.

There's an expression in our business. Every year, each barrel of whiskey loses about 4 percent due to evaporation. Goes up in the sky, disappears. We call that the angel's share. When Booker passed, the word around the distillery was that the angel's share doubled. That made sense, I thought. They got one big angel up there and I imagine he's always pretty thirsty.

I miss my father; be a liar if I said I didn't. Think about him every day. Booker. My dad. Yes, sir.

Booker, he taught me things, or tried to at least. About being fair, about being honest. About remembering who you were, and where you came from. About doing things right. To be sure, he had a temper, but in the end, he was a fair man, didn't hold a grudge. Had a heart, could be generous.

He taught me about my family, the grandfathers, the uncles, the cousins, our legacy and our responsibility to it. He also taught me about bourbon, how to make it the right way, how to preserve the process. How to stay focused, how to stay humble. He also taught me the importance of hard work, how there's no substitute for it. I try to remember what he said, try to do things the way he taught me. I hope I'm not letting him down. And I hope I can pass some of those things on to my own son, Freddie.

BOURBON PRIMER

The Beams' Bourbons

We're known worldwide for Jim Beam Bourbon, the famous whiskey with the white label that has little pictures of the seven generations of Beams on it. That's our flagship, the franchise player. We sell a lot of it, more than six million cases per year around the world. From Hardin Creek to Japan, it's been quite a ride.

But we sell a lot more than just Jim Beam Bourbon. The following list are our different bourbons, with some facts and

(*continued*)

(*continued*)

tasting notes. There will be no quiz on this information, and they are in no particular order. Read up if you want!

Jim Beam® Bourbon: The big dog and the one that started it all. A little bit sweet with a touch of caramel, this is a clean, crisp bourbon with a gentle snap. Bottled at 80 proof, and aged four years—twice as long as we have to, I might add. Good in your glass with some ice, or mixed with anything from a cola to a chocolate milkshake (try that sometime and thank me later), this whiskey was built to last and it has.

Jim Beam Black®: This 86-proof bourbon has the same recipe as our flagship brand, but it's aged longer (eight years in the United States). It's those extra years getting to know the wood that gives it a full-bodied flavor with smooth caramel and warm oak notes. It's meant to be sipped and savored. Good front porch whiskey.

Old Grand-Dad®: An historic bourbon, been around since 1882. Specifically formulated with more rye for a lighter, spicier flavor, lately it's been experiencing something of a renaissance, especially with younger consumers. Comes in various proofs, so you have your choice. Suggestion: they're all good, so you can't go wrong. Good straight up, but also makes for a nice cocktail, especially an old-fashioned.

Old Crow®: Another piece of history, this whiskey was the creation of a Scottish chemist turned distiller, Dr. James Crow, who worked for the Old Oscar Pepper Distillery in 1840. Aged four years and bottled at the standard 80 proof, it has a medium-light body and a short, sharp finish. Some more history: Dr. Crow invented or at least popularized the sour mash method, the process of using a little of yesterday's mash with today's. This ensured consistency in the whiskey. This process helped revolutionize whiskey making. We bought this bourbon in the late eighties.

Knob Creek®: Aged nine years in charred, American white oak barrels and bottled at an honest 100 proof, this whiskey has a maple sugar aroma and is a little sweet, woody and rich to the taste. I like all bourbons, but I like this a lot. If you're a fan of Manhattan cocktails, this brand works especially well as the main ingredient.

Knob Creek® Single Barrel Reserve: This bourbon is carefully hand selected, barrel-by-barrel. Aged nine years, and bottled at 120 proof, it has a little kick to it. But it's smooth and has a nice wood and vanilla flavor and aroma. It's easy sipping all the way.

Basil Hayden's®: This is one of the original Small Batch Bourbons, so it's been around for a while. Aged eight years, and bottled at a somewhat mild 80 proof, it uses twice as much rye in the recipe. The result is a slightly peppery taste and aroma with some honey mixed in. It has a gentle bite, so it can be enjoyed neat or in a cocktail. It's your call.

Baker's®: I've got a soft spot for this Small Batch Bourbon because it's named after my cousin, Baker Beam, who spent most of his life working at the distillery, then when he retired, he bought a house next door to it. Aged seven years and bottled at 107 proof, it's full bodied and has good balance. When you drink it, you'll probably pick up some fruit and caramel tastes. If you like cognac, you'll like this whiskey. It's won all sorts of awards.

(continued)

(*continued*)

Booker's®: One of the first ever ultra-premium brands, Booker's was the creation of the man it's named after. (I think I've already mentioned that.) It's still one of the only uncut, unfiltered, straight-from-the-barrel bourbons available today. Nothing is added to it: no water, no filters. What's in the barrel ends up in your mouth. Has a big oak nose and a pretty intense flavor that includes tobacco and fruit. Aged between six to eight years, it's bottled anywhere from 124 to 130 proof, so it's not to be fooled with. (The high proof allows you to add your own amount of water to your drink and lower the proof you want. Booker was big on that.) An honest Small Batch Bourbon from my dad. Probably should have listed this one first since it started a big trend.

Red Stag by Jim Beam®: The first flavor-infused bourbon from Jim Beam, this four-year-old, 80-proof whiskey comes in three distinct flavors: Black Cherry, Honey Tea, and Spiced.) More flavors, more choices. This is a good example of some of the new thinking we and the entire bourbon industry are embracing.

Devil's Cut®: This one might need a little more explaining because it's made a different way. When bourbon is dumped out of the barrel, a certain amount of whiskey is left trapped in the wood. We use a special process to extract that bourbon, pull it out. The name plays off the notion of the angel's share that I already mentioned. Bottled at 90 proof, it has a bold and woody taste and nose with some vanilla mixed in. Top-shelf stuff. (I get into a little more detail on this bourbon later on.)

4

COLLEGE MAN

Let's rewind now and go back to my college days, because they were a special part of my life—at least the part I remember. At Western Kentucky University, I majored in partying. Early colonial partying. Postmodern partying. Neoclassical partying. Political science partying. Economics 101 partying. I really took to the subject over in Bowling Green, really got into it with a passion and an interest, and my grade point showed it: 0.08—still an NCAA record.

I always thought the people who filmed the movie *Animal House* had secretly based the movie around me and my buds. I can't and won't get into a lot of old stories since the statute of limitations in Kentucky hasn't run out on some of the things I did back then. Let's just say I was always one step ahead of trouble.

If being a Beam drew attention at military school, that attention doubled in college. I had gone to Western with a number of local friends and soon made a lot more. You couldn't have a party without inviting Freddie Noe, Jim Beam's great-grandson; you knew I wouldn't come empty handed.

I took a lot of road trips back then, mostly to Nashville or Memphis. Once, Booker made the serious mistake of loaning me his Cadillac (all Beams eventually drive Cadillacs; I may be the first one not to), and about nine of my college buddies piled in and off we went, left Bowling Green in the dust. We put more than 3,000 miles on that vehicle in four weeks. We drove the wheels off that thing and when I came back, Booker checked the mileage and then blew a major gasket. So much smoke was pouring out of his ears, I could barely see his face.

"Where the hell did you drive to, boy? *Mars?*"

I shrugged and got the hell out of the kitchen. Truthfully, I really wasn't sure where I had been. Those three weeks were kind of a blur. One place I know I wasn't, though—class.

Most of my academic efforts in freshmen year centered around trying to persuade the Dean of Something, an old, little woman who could barely see over her desk, from kicking me out of school. I clearly remember one particular attempt.

"You never go to class, Mr. Noe," she said, peering over a pile of books through Coke-bottle glasses.

"Please, call me Fred. May I call you Edwina? That's a very beautiful name. My mom Annis's name is Edwina. Lovely name."

"You never go to class!"

"Well, Edwina, the truth is I'm too busy doing homework. I can't do both."

"This is unacceptable and I don't think we can tolerate this much longer."

I looked down at the floor, tried to make eyes well up, which was easy because they were already bloodshot having been up all night. "I will redouble my efforts, ma'am," I said.

"You better, young man!"

"Yes ma'am." I got up to leave, then turned back around. If it worked at military school, it might work here. "Excuse me, ma'am, but I happen to have in my possession a case of bourbon. It was sent to me by accident, I think. It's in the trunk of my car right out front. Jim Beam Bourbon, best-selling bourbon in the world. I'm Jim Beam's great-grandson, by the way. Don't know if you know that or are familiar with him. By any chance, you wouldn't have a need for some of America's Native Spirit, would you? Aged four years, and bottled a real nice drinkable 80 proof. Pretty copper color and nice nose. It's all yours to enjoy. I have an endless supply, not that that matters."

Edwina looked at me like she had just stepped in something.

"If not for you, ma'am, then maybe for the man in your life? Makes for a nice present."

She pointed to the door behind me. "Get out of my office right now, Mr. Noe. Right now."

"I'm leaving, ma'am. Heading straight to the library, yes I am. Going to read every book in it even if it takes all morning."

As (bad) luck would have it, Booker had the honor of telling me my college career at Western had come to an ignominious conclusion. We were sitting at the kitchen table having supper over winter break when he casually asked me where I was going to go to school the next semester. At first I was confused, then suddenly I wasn't. I remembered grades were due out any day. I stared down at my dinner, thought if this was my last meal on earth, I would have preferred something other than meatloaf and carrots. I pushed my plate away from me. I had meant to get home to check the mail that day, get to the mailbox before Booker did, take the initiative, but had gotten involved in a little card game instead.

"Western," I said. I stared at my meat loaf like it was the most interesting thing in the world. "Western Kentucky University, that is."

"You think so, huh?"

"Yes, sir. Eager to get back to the books."

Booker gave me one of his "How dumb do you think I am, boy?" looks, then slowly nodded and slid a letter across the table. The letter was short and left little for interpretation:

I was no longer a student at Western Kentucky University due to academic infractions. I was pretty sure Edwina had hand-delivered that note that morning.

"Must be some kind of mistake," I said.

"I think I'm looking at the mistake," Booker said.

I studied the letter, saw my grade point average, saw a whole lot of zeroes. "I'll fix this."

"Looks like you've already been fixed, boy," Booker said. (Full disclosure: That's a *highly* a sanitized version of what he actually said. What transpired at that kitchen table for the next hour is best not repeated.)

"Yes, sir," I said when the father-son pep talk was over. "I'll start researching new schools tomorrow, maybe even tonight. Get right on it."

Well, I didn't get right on anything. Booker did. He was two steps ahead of me. That afternoon, he had already gotten me an application for St. Catherine Junior College, which was nearby, as well as a job working at Toddy's Liquor Store in downtown Bardstown.

Toddy's was an institution in town. It was part liquor store, part bar—and all Kentucky. It had a strong and regular clientele, a colorful group of men I got to know pretty well. It was owned by Toddy Beam, who was a cousin of mine six-and-a-half times removed. (We never figured out how we were related. As I have said, there are a lot of Beams in Kentucky and the family tree is long and the branches tangled. I'm sure if we each had a month, we could have figured it out.)

Cousin Toddy was short and squat like a whiskey barrel and he was always griping or moaning or fussing about something: business, the weather, Notre Dame football, politics, being on his feet all day and all night. He was also a neat freak; he was constantly dusting or sweeping or mopping. Even though Toddy's wasn't exactly the bar at the Waldorf, I have to admit it was spotless. Toddy was always running a rag over something, making things shine. He was proud of the place. It was his life.

I worked six nights a week, tending bar and stocking the shelves. As you can imagine, I wasn't thrilled with the whole situation: living at home, working a few blocks away, going to a community college during the day, Booker watching my every move. I was a trapped rat and regretted what had transpired at Western. I had had a good thing going in college, freedom, but I had blown it and was back where I started. The first few weeks in my new life were tough, but after some thought, I decided, what the hell, might as well make the best of the situation. So I gave it a go, worked hard at something for once. Besides, I didn't have a whole lot of options; I was flat broke and needed the paycheck.

Eventually, things got better and much to my surprise, I actually started liking my job. Down deep, Toddy was a good old boy, had a real heart, and the regulars—and there were a lot of them—were funny and entertaining boys. Everyone had a story to tell, everyone had a joke. Most of them were working men, ducking out to grab a shot and a beer before heading back home to the wife and kids. Wednesday night was a big night in Bardstown because that's when the *Kentucky Standard*, the weekly newspaper, came out. The men would use that as an excuse to get out of the house. "Going out to get the paper, be right back." Then they'd hustle down to Toddy's, do a little drinking and razz on Toddy, who was always telling them to watch their cigarette ashes. ("A bar ain't an ash tray! How many times I gotta tell you?")

I would get a lot of calls from pissed-off wives on Wednesday night. At first I did my best to cover for my customers. I was young and respectful of them.

"Fred, It's Shirley Bekins. Is Eddie there?"

I'd be staring square at Eddie Bekins, elbows on the bar, head in glass.

"No, ma'am."

"You sure?"

"Yes, ma'am. He's definitely not here."

"You positive?"

"One hundred percent. No sign of Eddie. You might want to check church, I think there's bingo tonight."

That all changed one night.

"Fred? This is Betsy Watkins. Is Tommy there?"

"No, ma'am."

"You sure?"

"Yes, ma'am."

"You're positive?"

"I'm positive, ma'am. He's definitely not here."

"So, there's no one there with a beer gut, a UK sweat-shirt, and a sorry ass?"

That description could have fit just about everyone in Toddy's. "No, ma'am. No one here like that."

"Well, Fred, I think you're full of *shit*, because I'm in the phone booth across the street and I can see him sitting right across the bar from you."

I looked out the window. Sure enough, there was sweet Betsy inside the phone booth. When she stepped outside and gave me the finger, I quietly hung up the phone. "Last call, brother," I said to Tommy. "Time to get back to your little princess."

After that, my motto was, "If you're here, you're here." And I stuck with it. I had enough trouble in my life. I didn't need any more from The Wives of Bardstown, Kentucky.

I also didn't need any trouble from the FBI. Toddy's was rumored to have been a place where a man could place a bet or two. Legend had it that it had been raided some years before, but I could never verify it. Toddy was mum on the subject, as were the regulars. Code of silence when it came to that issue. But every so often, someone from out of town would come in and want to lay some money down. Put it on a horse, bet against the spread of the UK game. I never knew what to do and when I asked Toddy, he would get more agitated than usual, tell me to throw them out, say he didn't know what the hell they were talking about, that he ran a legitimate business, and storm away to mop up the back room. My guess was there was a time where you could get more than a drink there, but those times had changed and Toddy, whether it he liked it or not, was now on the up and up.

I worked at Toddy's for more than three years, and as I said, I can't say I didn't like it. When it was slow, I did my studying. I had finished up at St. Catherine and was now attending Bellarmine University in Louisville during the day. But while I was working on my degree, I was getting my real education every night. In a lot of ways, my job at Toddy's helped prepare me for my future.

It was there that I learned how to get along with people, listen to them, humor them, entertain them. It was at that small liquor store and bar on the west side of town that I got to see working men up close, hear their life stories, their hopes, their disappointments. I saw how hard work can make a man, but could also break one.

I also saw what alcohol could do to you, how too much of a good thing could turn bad. How having "one for the road" wasn't a good idea. Oddly enough, it was while working at a bar that I first learned the lesson of drinking smart, in moderation.

I also learned about Kentucky, my home state. Even though there were mostly Bardstown regulars in Toddy's, a lot of people from other areas dropped in to buy packaged liquor on their way somewhere. Coal miners from the eastern part of the state, horse people from Lexington, city and bourbon people from Louisville. Someone once said

Kentucky is like three states in one, since every region is so different. The mountains in the east, the bluegrass and horse farms in the center, the Ohio River and hills (or knobs, as we call them) in the west. But there are common traits, I noticed, things that tie all Kentuckians together. Honesty. Humility. A work ethic. An ability to roll with whatever life gives you. And a sense of humor. More than anything, I think we've got that.

We have a lot to be proud of in Kentucky. For a small state, we produce the world's best whiskey, the fastest horses, and a lot of multimillionaire basketball players thanks to the University of Kentucky (all right, and sometimes Louisville).

What really sets us apart, though, is the priority we put on family and friends. They come first. Always have, always will. When you get right down to it, Kentucky is like one big small town. Everyone seems to know everyone, everyone seems to be pulling for each other. When someone from Kentucky makes it, we all make it. We kind of have a permanent underdog thing going, an us-against-them mentality. We're not East Coast, we're not West Coast, we're not Midwest, and despite how we talk, we're not really even South. We are who we are. A hilly little state that's been around longer than most, full of tough but decent people. And it was Toddy's, a shoebox of a bar in my hometown, that first made me see and appreciate that. Strange where you can learn things.

After I got my degree in business administration, I immediately put it to good use by hitting the road with Hank Williams, Jr. and his band. Hank was something of a family friend back then, Booker knew and liked him, and the company (per my original suggestion, I like to point out) had started sponsoring him because, at the time, he was a devoted consumer of our product.

The family wasn't thrilled with my decision. I finally had a college degree, I was part of a prominent family, and here I was running around with a band. But I wanted to get out of Bardstown, spread my wings, do something different. I knew the distillery was there and that the ghosts were waiting for me, but I wasn't sure I wanted that life. Truthfully, I wasn't sure what I wanted, so I hit the road and hit it hard.

I actually didn't spend all that much time with Hank. I spent most of my time with his band. I was the jack of all trades for them, doing this, doing that. In addition to my primary job, making sure everyone was well provisioned with bourbon, I helped the roadies haul and set up gear. Sometimes I played security guard, kept the fans away from Hank, or helped his manager collect and count the money from the promoter. (They always paid in cash.)

When I wasn't working, I was having a big time in whatever town we rolled into. We were a mobile party, I'll tell you that. The bus had Hank's name on the outside, so everyone knew who we were. We could stop in the middle of a desert in the middle of the night and within minutes, there would be girls pounding on the doors of the bus, wanting in. We obliged every time.

I loved the life, no doubt about that—this was as close as I was ever going to get to being a rock star—so I did it off and on for a few years, soaking it all up. I don't remember too many specifics about those times, to be honest, just bits and pieces: sleeping on the bus with the boys, eating in coffee shops, passing the bottle around before and after the concert. I remember one night, after the show, Dixie, the piano player (a man named Dixie could only play in a band), pulled out a gun and shot out the TV in our hotel room. I guess he couldn't find the remote. I remember another: sitting on the floor of the bus, counting piles of twenty-dollar bills from the last show and sticking it all in a big brown paper bag when I was done, like I had just robbed a bank. Like I said, bits and pieces of memories swirling around.

It was in Paris, Tennessee, when Hank asked me to officially work for him. We were in a parking lot shooting off hand-engraved pistols that he had just given everyone for Christmas (he was pretty creative in the gift-giving department; no ties or fruit cakes from him) when he asked if I wanted to be the band's road manager. Up until that point, I had more or less been freelancing, working in an unofficial capacity, getting paid here and there under the table. But now, though, hell, I might even get a business card, maybe even a W-2 form.

This was close to a dream come true. Life on the road. Seeing the world. Girls, partying, music. And a regular paycheck. This wasn't some garage band. Hank was a huge star, his career off the charts. He was playing to sold-out crowds around the country and making music videos. (One of his videos, "Young Country," even starred Booker. It won top country music video of the year two years in a row.) I could latch on to Hank's tail and ride it for a while. I was in my mid-twenties, hadn't seen much of the world, if anything (when I traveled with the band in my unofficial capacity, it had been pretty much been in Kentucky and Tennessee), so I was happy with the offer.

But then the damnedest thing happened. Instead of saying yes, I told the band that I had to think about it for a few days, and I did. I'm not the most introspective person in the world—usually I do what my gut tells me, try not to overthink things—but I was conflicted. While life helping to manage a big band was appealing, down deep, I knew I had another calling; down deep, something was pulling me in another direction. I called Booker, told him about the offer, and asked for his advice.

"That ain't no life for you, boy," he said. "Maybe we can finally find something for you at the plant."

I think there comes a time in everyone's life when you have to look in the mirror, take stock of who you are, where you're going, and make a decision on what direction you should head in. Crossroads, they call them. Some people might come to them just once in their lives, others a few times. Regardless, they're important, and most likely, the decisions are hard.

I thought about what Booker had said and I knew he was right. Working for Hank was no life for me. I was no rock star. I called Booker back, told him I wanted a job. It was time to go home. I was a Beam, and Beams make bourbon.

BOURBON PRIMER

How to Taste Bourbon

Since you now know how to make bourbon the right way, I guess it would only be right to know how to taste it the right way. All you need is a nose, a mouth, and a glass. Hell, sometimes you don't even need a glass. A bottle will do just fine.

But to do it right, get a glass and pour yourself a shot. (Don't overdo it now; we're tasting, not drinking.) Take a look at its color, assess it. All bourbons are brown, of course; as I pointed out, they get that color from aging inside the barrel. As a general rule, the darker a bourbon is, the more complex in flavor and the higher proof it is. So if it's dark, batten down the hatches.

Next, swirl the bourbon a bit to aerate it, mix it up with the air and let it breathe, then put your nose deep into the glass and inhale deeply. Make sure you keep your lips parted when you do this, that's key. This way, you'll taste the bourbon before you actually taste it; you'll feel it floating around in your mouth. You're going to smell different things when you do this: honey, tobacco, wood, fruit. Everyone is going to detect something different, and it's all good.

After you've done that, it's time to taste it. Now the tongue has different taste points: the tip of it detects

Jim Beam and family in front of the Big House on North Third Street in Bardstown, Kentucky, pre-1913. From left to right: Jim Beam, T. Jeremiah Beam, Maw Maw Beam, Margaret Beam Noe (my grandmother), family friend visiting the day the photo was taken, Mildred Beam, and David M. Beam.

Courtesy of Beam Inc.

Jim Beam standing in front of his office at the distillery after the repeal of Prohibition.

Courtesy of Beam Inc.

Jim Beam cuts cake in celebration of the distillery's reopening after Prohibition in 1935.

Courtesy of Beam Inc.

In the 1940s, Jim Beam hit the road hard promoting the brand. Here he is standing near the Michigan Avenue Bridge in Chicago.

Courtesy of Beam Inc.

Me around two years old—probably on my way to a party somewhere. Here comes the seventh generation! (1959)

Courtesy of Jim Beam Family.

Brothers David (front) and Baker Beam pose for an ad that appeared in *Playboy* magazine. (circa 1969)

Courtesy of Beam Inc.

Dad and my cousin Baker, on a pond at the distillery, posing for another *Playboy* ad.

Courtesy of Beam Inc.

The Beam "whiskey men" pose for an official picture in 1965. Left to right: Carl, his sons, David and Baker; Booker; and Uncle Jere.

Courtesy of Beam Inc.

From left to right: Carl Beam, T. Jeremiah Beam, Booker Noe, and Baker Beam at the distillery in the early 1970s.

Courtesy of Beam Inc.

Graduating eighth grade from the Castle Heights Military Academy, private first class, in 1971. I'm sure they were glad to see me leave.

Courtesy of Jim Beam Family.

Me putting on my game face before a game at the Academy in Lebanon, Tennessee. (1974)

Courtesy of Jim Beam Family.

BELLARMINE COLLEGE
1982

Five colleges, seven years, and finally a graduation from Bellarmine University! I loved school so much I never wanted to leave. I guess you could say I was "thirsty" for knowledge. (1982)

Courtesy of Jim Beam Family.

Hank Williams, Jr. with Booker at the Beam distillery in the late 1980s. Don't know what they were talking about but it looks pretty important.

Courtesy of Jim Beam Family.

Booker holding one of his prized smoked hams in 1995.

Courtesy of Beam Inc.

My mom, Annis, and Booker at "Bourbon Fest," an annual celebration in Bardstown, in the early 1990s.

Courtesy of Jim Beam Family.

My dad, Booker—Yes, sir! (1998)

Courtesy of Beam Inc.

Booker, family friend Toogie (center), and my mom around the famous kitchen table. We sampled a lot of bourbon at that table over the years. (1999)

Courtesy of Jim Beam Family.

Father and son, an official portrait. (2002)

Courtesy of Beam Inc.

Getting ready to lead a tasting on the distillery grounds in Clermont. (2005)

Courtesy of Beam Inc.

Family is everything. Pictured here is Sandy, Freddie, and me at Bourbon Fest 2010.

Courtesy of Beam Inc.

Jim, the PR guy, and me at a bourbon tasting in our backyard in 2005.

Courtesy of JSHA Public Relations.

Me with the bronze statue of Dad, which was unveiled in front of the T. Jeremiah Beam Home at the Clermont plant in September 2005 to honor his legacy.

Courtesy of Beam Inc.

Pensive pose at the distillery, my second home. Been pretty much everywhere, but this is my favorite spot. (2007)

Courtesy of Jim Beam Family.

Generations seven and eight at the 2008 Indianapolis 500.

Courtesy of Beam Inc.

Me and my buds, Eddie Montgomery (left) and Troy Gentry, backstage in 2009.

Courtesy of Jim Beam Family.

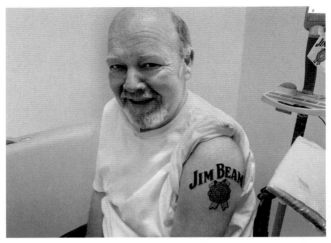

The famous tattoo! I got it in response to our loyal fans' requests. (2011)

Courtesy of Beam Inc.

Me peering over the shoulder of Matt Shattock, President & CEO, Beam Inc., at the closing of the New York Stock Exchange in October 2011.

Courtesy of Beam Inc.

An evening with Kid Rock is always a big time. (Detroit, 2012)

Photo Credit © Joe Vaughn.

An inside look at one of our rack houses. This is where the magic happens—where bourbon is aged.

Courtesy of Beam Inc.

The T. Jeremiah Beam Home at the Clermont distillery. A number of Beams lived in this house while working at the plant.

Courtesy of Beam Inc.

One of our nine-story rack houses at our Clermont, Kentucky, plant.

Courtesy of Beam Inc.

Kentucky, the Bluegrass State and Beam homeland.

Courtesy of www.kentuckytourism.com.

sweetness, the sides spices, and the center is pretty much neutral. So you want to involve your whole mouth in the process. The best way to do that is to take a sip and move it around the sides of your mouth, work it hard, chew it a little. We call this the Kentucky Chew. So chew it a little, then swallow it. Depending on what you're drinking, you're going to taste different things. More fruit, some wood, some sugar, a little fire. Once again, all good—especially if it's one of our bourbons.

There's people out there, spirit writers, smart people who taste whiskey for a living and write about what they taste. (Hell, I thought *I* had a good job.) While many of them are my friends, I have to admit, I think they sometimes go too far in trying to describe a bourbon. I've seen bourbons described as tasting like "new-mown grass" and "soot." Terms like that don't exactly resonate with me. (How many times have you tasted soot?) But they're professionals, and I guess they know what they're doing, so I'll let them do their job.

When I lead a tasting, I try not to "overdescribe" the bourbons to the people in the audience. I think taste is an individual thing; everyone detects something different and I don't want to influence them with my "expert opinion." It's up to you if you taste honey, grass, or soot. (If you taste all three at the same time, you're drinking one weird bourbon. . . .)

A few other tasting notes: if you're tasting a few bourbons, start with the lowest proof first and gradually make your way up to the highest proof. This way you won't be shocking your taste buds. Also, when you're done tasting one bourbon, make sure you have a sip of water or a bite of a unflavored cracker to clean your palette before moving on

(continued)

(continued)

to the next sample. One more final note: you should initially taste your bourbons straight up, or "neat," to get their full aroma and flavor. After you're done, you should then add a splash or two of bottled water. (Try to avoid tap water if you can; as we say, the chlorine don't do the bourbon proud.)

The final step in the tasting process is to assess "the finish." This is kind of a fancy way to say how the bourbon feels in your throat or stomach—the lingering sensation it creates—after you swallowed it. Some bourbons have a long finish, they stay with you, others have a short one, there and gone. A lot of the finish is determined by the age and proof. Usually, the higher proof, the longer the finish, but once again, it's an individual thing, so it's your call.

5

STARTING OUT

I started on the bottling line. Clermont plant. Night shift. Relief supervisor. In other words, they didn't put my picture on the bottle right away. It wasn't glamorous, and I was on my feet a lot. I remember wondering after my first night what Hank and the boys were up to, where they were. A couple of weeks earlier, I had been partying in Nashville, living the life; now I was in a hot and noisy room watching bottles whirl around on an assembly line. Four PM to 1 AM. Sometimes 4 PM to 4 AM. Half hour for lunch or whatever it is you eat at 10 at night.

Luke, this is your destiny

I need to be clear on one thing here: nobody, not Booker or my cousins, nobody forced me to come work for the business. Despite the legacy, despite the generations of Beams working there, no one pressured me, or even encouraged me for that matter, to go make whiskey. Booker in particular was very impartial on the subject. He wanted me to make up my own mind, be my own man.

"The distillery's not for everyone," he told me when I came back from the road. We were sitting at the kitchen table, waiting on breakfast from Mom.

"I know that."

"Last time. You sure you want to do this?"

"Yes, sir."

"Why?"

I admit, since I had returned home, I had been asking myself that question *a lot*. And I came up with an honest answer: "Because I think this is supposed to be what I do. This is what I know."

Booker looked hard at me. "You know, this isn't a party. No Hank Williams, Jr. It's work. Hard work."

"Yes, sir."

He kind of chewed on his bottom lip, mulled things over. Booker was big into mulling. "All right," he said. "We're going to do it right then. You going to learn it from the ground up."

That was the reason he started me in the bottling house (where we filled bottles with liquor). It was the only part of the business he didn't know. Booker had never worked there, so he had never been able to teach me much about it. It was a gap in my education, as he put it, so that's where my bourbon career officially started.

I can't say I loved it at first. It wasn't the most interesting job. Plus, the other workers there were wary of me; polite but distant. I found out later they thought I was a spy. Jim Beam's great-grandson, checking up on them, ready to report back. But after a while, they saw that I was one of them, just another guy making a living. No special treatment. Bring my lunch bucket, just like them. Pretty soon, once they realized I wasn't tape-recording their conversations or taking notes and running back to Booker, they relaxed.

I remember the night they officially accepted me into the fold. I was on the bottling line overseeing a run of margarita mix (while we only make bourbon at the distillery, we sometimes bottle other products there before we ship them out) when one of the older guys, a mechanic, told me there was a problem with one of the palletizing machines and I needed to check it out right away. I had nothing to do with the maintenance of the palletizing machines, and I told him that.

"Just go on now, go down there and check it out. Something needs your attention. Get your ass back here when you're done."

So I went over to one of machines off in the corner, and sure enough, there was the thing that needed my attention: a cold, tall margarita, waiting for me. I picked up that glass, turned around, and toasted my coworkers, then threw that thing back fast. From that moment on, I was just one of the boys.

I ended up liking the work. It was important, and it was straightforward. I liked the fact that we were some of the last people to see our bourbons before they were shipped off to points around the world.

Every so often, I got to do something that made a difference. After I moved over to the labeling room, I soon learned that we needed a system to track which cases were going where. So I came up with a code that we would put on each label before we put it on a bottle. Eventually it became known as the "F. Noe Code" and we used it for years, until computers came along. I was proud of that code. Made me think I had an impact.

We had some interesting situations pop up in the labeling room, things that kept us scrambling. During that time we were expanding overseas, shipping our product to Australia, Germany, Japan, South Africa, and Russia. We had to come up with different labels for the different countries, and in some cases we weren't sure what we were putting on the label. No one spoke Japanese in the shipping department in Clermont, so we had to call over to Tokyo and ask our local sales contact how to spell "bourbon." In South Africa, we learned that we couldn't use the word "proof" on our labels; apparently it was a derogatory term down there.

Another interesting situation: We used massive containers to ship our products. We sent them overseas to Russia or the Far East full and they would come back empty on ships. Well, supposedly empty. More than once, workers unloading the containers in Europe found people, whole families hiding in them, stowaways, trying to sneak into the West free of charge. Like I said, interesting situations.

So the work could be more challenging than it sounds, and I ended up liking it all right. I suppose I also liked the routine. After years of excess, years of partying, years of no real direction (case in point: I took seven years to graduate college), I finally found my footing at the distillery, felt earth beneath my feet. Like I said, it wasn't glamorous work, but it was honest work and it helped me grow up.

I mostly liked the people I worked with. They were solid people who had worked at the plant for years and years. Many of their fathers had worked there, and even some of their grandfathers. The Beams, I realized, weren't the only family with bourbon-making roots. Bourbon and Beam had supported generations of Kentuckians for years and years. It was in a lot of families' blood.

Sometimes, after work, we would meet at the bottom of the hill in the parking lot (the Clermont plant is built on a hill) and we would relax and have us a few. No crazy stuff, just sipping and smoking. Someone might be playing guitar, someone might be singing. We'd sit there on the bumpers of our cars or in the back of our trucks and watch the night fade, see the sun come up over the hills, the light hitting the rack houses, turning them pink, then a little orange. I remember staring up at the rack house, wondering what time the ghosts got up, wondering what they thought of me—the prodigal—now.

We drank our share of whiskey, but we didn't overdo it. We were professionals; it was all about quality, not so much quantity. (Although, to be sure, there were a few who were into both, but they didn't last too long; they tended to weed themselves out.) We were selective of what we drank, knew where the best whiskey was stored, which rack houses, which barrels.

Sometimes we sipped on new whiskey, bourbon that hadn't been aged yet. White Dog, clear as water, but dangerously seductive too. Drink too much of that and the next morning you would wake up with an earthquake between your ears. Bust Head, Booker called it. "You got the Bust Head," he would say.

Some of the workers, the old-timers especially, had something called a "mule." It was a distillery secret, no outsiders knew about it. It was basically a plastic tube that you could hide down the front of your overalls. You would pull it out in the rack houses if no one was around, knock out the bung of a barrel (the plug), and slip it on in and have yourself a nightcap, or an afternoon pick-me-up, or a fat-free breakfast.

There was a trick to knowing which barrels to sip from. Since the barrels were aged for years and years, they naturally picked up their share of dust as they sat quietly, undisturbed in the shadows. But every so often you would come across a barrel with no dust on one side, and that's the one you put your mule in. The reason they didn't have any dust on them was because the men (many of whom had, shall we say, prominent stomachs) would lean against the barrel while sipping on it. Their guts kind of shined the barrel up. Those barrels were called the sweet barrels. The shinier the barrel, the sweeter the whiskey. I always thought we should come out with a special bourbon, call it "Shiny Barrel." I know it would sell well in Kentucky. People who knew their whiskey would know what it was all about and line up to buy it for sure.

I worked at the distillery for 28 years, moving around the place, serving in a number of capacities. As Booker wanted, I was learning the family business from the ground up, all aspects. Bottling, labeling, the distillery, the fermenting room, the dump room. My knowledge of the business grew inch by inch, day by day. Looking back on it, I was like a bourbon myself, aging slowly, gaining flavor in the relative quiet of the Clermont plant.

Age and experience are important things in the bourbon industry. You can't learn everything in one day, or one week, or even a year, especially in a business as old as ours. It takes time to absorb all the different facets and it takes patience to learn the nuances. There is a rhythm to making whiskey, it's a slow, easy, and methodical process. This isn't Silicon Valley where things change every day. This isn't Wall Street with the big ups and downs. This is Bullit County,

Clermont, Kentucky; things may change here, but when they do, they change slow.

I was content enough. By then I had met up with a girl who would later become my wife. I had met her driving "the loop" in Bardstown. The loop was a Saturday or summer evening ritual, and you've probably seen it in movies about small towns. Bunch of people pile up in a car and drive around. We started out at Burger Queen (that's not a typo; in Bardstown, we had a Burger Queen; not sure why) and ended up about a mile away at the McDonald's. Then we'd drive back again. It usually turned into a parade of cars, people honking their horns, the radios up high, seeing what's going on. Teenagers did it, people in their twenties did it. Bardstown is a little isolated; there aren't many other towns really close by, Louisville is close to an hour away and Lexington even further, so our entertainment options were limited. It was either drive the loop, or sit on someone's front porch and watch people drive the loop.

Well, I met Sandy driving the loop, and we started hanging out and then going to ballgames, and later, the local night spot, Boots and Bourbon, and one thing led to another and pretty soon we were married and pretty soon, man, I was a father.

It was all good. Sandy was a Bardstown girl, so she had a basic understanding of the bourbon business, knew what it meant to be a Beam, so there was no major education needed. She knew that bourbon, whiskey making, was going to be my life and she was fine with that. She understood she wasn't marrying a doctor or a lawyer. I tell you, having a spouse who is on board with your career, someone who gets it, that's a big help. And Sandy got it from the start and she's been there the whole time.

So I was all settled down and everything, Hank Williams, Jr. and that life, gone forever, the transgressions of my youth a memory. The days blended together, one after another, and my life kind of flattened out, no real highs and no real lows. I was happy enough. I had everything a man could want: a good wife; a son, Freddie (Frederick Booker Noe IV; we like to number our kids); a good job working with good people. Family nearby. Sandy and I were living in the Small House, next to Booker and my mom. I told myself that was enough

But I knew it wasn't, knew something was missing. Down deep, I felt an itch to do something different, an itch to see the world. I didn't leave Bardstown or Kentucky very often, it was pretty much my whole world, so that itch was understandable and over time it grew.

Booker was gone a lot, traveling, seeing new things, meeting new people, while he promoted the product. It was the 1990s and the Small Batch Bourbons, particularly Knob Creek, were on fire, demand high. When he came back, we would sit around the kitchen table, maybe sample a few batches of Booker's the distillery had sent over, and he would tell stories about Australia, Japan, France. Places I could only dream about. That itch would get stronger after talking to Booker, but I ignored it, told myself to be happy with how things had turned out.

Things changed one day, though, when Booker came home from some faraway place tired. Being the ambassador for one of the world's most recognizable brands, being the face of a growing and global company, being here and being there, constantly entertaining people, key customers, retailers, salespeople, media, was finally taking a toll. He was pushing 70 by then, and the front porch was calling.

"I'm done," he said. We were sitting out back, staring at the smokehouse, waiting on supper. When Booker was in town, we still tried to eat together. "I don't want to do this anymore."

I just sat there and let him blow off steam. He had complained about life on the road before, so I didn't think much of this latest tirade about airports and too-small seats on airplanes. He had recently spent time in Japan and had to push two beds together to sleep, which he thought an outrage.

"You can't quit," I said.

"It's not quitting. They got a word for what I'm doing and it's called *retiring*. And that's what I'm doing. I am *retiring*. Ball players do it. Hell, even racehorses do it."

I wasn't taking him seriously. "You can't do that."

"I can do whatever I damn well please. I'm not getting on any more airplanes. That last trip almost killed me. Waiting in line at the airport for an hour and then they lost my suitcase. Besides, I ain't feeling too well. Gettin' swimmy headed. My legs and my feet are swelling up all the time. No, I'm done, all right, I'm done. Besides, they don't want to hear from an old man anymore anyway.

They want someone younger. A different perspective. I've told all my stories and I'm getting tired of hearing myself talk." He went quiet, started in on a good mulling. Then he softly said something.

"What?" I hadn't heard him.

"I said it's your turn."

"What do you mean?"

"What do you think I mean? This is your time. Changing of the guard. I already talked to people about it. They've been watching you for a while and the reports have all been pretty good. You put your time in here, so they're going give you a shot."

"A shot?"

"Yeah, a shot. Speaking of which, I'm getting a little thirsty." He pushed himself out of his chair and went into the house.

I watched him walk away. Time to scratch that itch, I thought.

BOURBON PRIMER

The Distillery

Since I spent so much of my life at our plant in Clermont, I thought it might be helpful to offer up a little description and a few definitions of the various parts of a working distillery. Every distillery is a little different, but they all have common terms and places, so in case you're interested or

(continued)

(*continued*)

you're ever in the neighborhood and want to stop by, here are a few:

- Fermenting room: A large building with 19 fermenting vats inside of it. This is where we add our secret and special family yeast and let it do its work: turning the mash into alcohol. The mash sits in these tubs for a few days, until it starts to bubble.

- The still: Ground zero, where it all happens. After it's been fermented, we take the mash and we run it through a column that's close to 200 degrees on the inside. This heat turns the alcohol into a gas or vapor. We then condense that, turn it back into a liquid. This newly distilled spirit is called Low Wine. Since the Low Wine still has a lot of impurities in it, we run it through something called the Doubler, which is really just another still, and produce something called High Wine. High Wine is colorless and looks like water and, as I've said, its nickname is White Dog. It's drinkable and it's probably what whiskey used to look and taste like 200 years ago, when my great-great-great-great-grandfather Jacob sold it, because they didn't have time to age it much.

- Cistern room: This is where the White Dog is filled into new, American oak barrels, which, by law, can only be used once. As I think I've mentioned, these barrels are burned or charred on the inside. Our bourbons get all of their color and a lot of their final taste and aroma through these barrels, so they're important. (When we're done with these barrels, we sell them off to scotch and tequila distilleries; that's why those spirits taste pretty good.) The bourbon goes into the barrel at no more than 125 proof. It's been cut a little with water to get it down to that level.

- Rack houses: After the cistern room, we send the barrels off to grow up in the rack houses. These are those large and spooky buildings I've mentioned, about nine stories high. This is where we age our bourbon. We don't heat our rack houses and we don't cool them, and we don't rotate the barrels that are inside of them either. We just put the barrels in there and leave them alone, let nature do its work. (PS. There aren't any ghosts up in them. At least none that have been documented.) Between our Clermont and Boston plants, we have more than 1.5 million barrels aging at any one time.

- Dump room: After the barrels are done aging, anywhere from four to nine years, we bring a bunch of them down and "dump" all the bourbon out, marrying it all together.

- Bottling line: This is where I started my illustrious career. It's a noisy and pretty big place where we fill bottles with our whiskey. We have a state-of-the-art bottling line, it's fast and it's efficient, and that's all you probably need to know.

If you come visit the distillery, we now offer guided tours that take you inside the distillery so you can see how we make our world famous whiskey; a tasting room where you can sample our bourbons in style; our American Stillhouse where you can learn more about our history (and maybe buy a few momentos . . .) and a smaller stillhouse where you can help make bourbon. All in all, a great experience.

(continued)

(continued)

Distillery Facts (Clermont and Booker Noe Plants)

- We make 115,000 gallons of whiskey a day.
- We put in 1,550 barrels in and out of the warehouses each day.
- We produce 400,000 barrels of bourbon a year.
- We have 1.6 million barrels in storage at any given time in our warehouses.

6

THE MAKING OF A
BOURBON AMBASSADOR

I started my education on becoming the company's Bourbon Ambassador by trying to learn the proper way to speak Southern. They flew up some expert speech coach from Atlanta to spend a day with me to help me do that. Apparently people in Atlanta speak a certain type of Southern that is acceptable to the rest of the world.

"I already know the proper way to speak Southern. Been doing it my whole life," I told Jim, the PR guy. I had inherited Jim from Booker, Booker had bequeathed him to me, and I could tell he was a little embarrassed about the whole thing.

"It's just to help you do your job," he said.

"Hell, what she going to teach me, the right way to say 'y'all'?"

"She's going to teach you how to talk more city Southern."

"City what?"

"City Southern."

"What do I talk now?"

"Country Southern."

"What the hell's the difference?"

"Well." Jim stood there and did his own mulling for a while before saying, "It's just one day, Fred. Come on. And we'll have a nice lunch. I'll order in from that place."

The City Southern session didn't go according to plan. The coach was an energetic woman who jumped up and down and waved her hands around like she was part of the landing crew of an aircraft carrier that was under attack. I'm sure she meant well, but I wasn't doing much to cooperate. I thought the whole thing ridiculous.

"You're dragging your words out," she said.

I looked at her. "That's how I talk."

"Condense your cadence."

"Condense my what?"

"Your cadence."

"What's a cadence?" I looked over at Jim, who pretended not to hear me. He was studying a menu from the restaurant we were going to order lunch from.

"Let's try again," the coach said, clapping her hands. "Speak from the diaphragm."

"My dia-what?"

We spent a good part of the day up at the Beam House at the distillery, the same house where my great Uncle Jere had lived, the same house where my cousins Carl and Baker and David had lived, trying to change the way I talked. I had generations of Country Southern in me; that wasn't changing anytime soon.

Finally, after a few hours of her trying to get me to condense my cadence, enunciate and articulate, and not drawl too much and not drag my words out and not say "ain't," and "y'all," and "reckon," she waved her hands one last time and gave up.

"Maybe we should get something to eat," she said.

"Good idea," Jim said. He suddenly perked up.

We ate lunch and I made a point of drawling a little bit more just to irritate her. Afterwards, the Southern speech coach quietly got back in her rental car and went back to the airport. I never saw her again.

"That didn't go quite like I envisioned," Jim said as she pulled out.

"Why, I reckon not."

The next step in my Bourbon Ambassador education was media training. Teach me what and what not to say to reporters and writers when I was being interviewed in case I was ever on *60 Minutes*. Jim was in charge of this. He had traveled with Booker for years, so he knew a lot about damage control.

We were at the distillery, back upstairs in the same room in the Beam House with a camera, PowerPoint, and message points. There was a little book they gave me, "The Do's and Don'ts" of talking with the media. ("Don't say, 'No comment.' Do use the reporter's first name. Don't drink on the air. Do show the bottle, label first, to the camera.") Jim and his crew instructed me on how to sit and hold my hands, and how it was important to remember not to cuss on live TV, and then how to sit and hold my hands some more. Then they filmed me and played it back on a TV so I could see how I held my hands and didn't cuss. The morning dragged on and on. I had every intention of taking my training seriously—bourbon, the process, the brands, the history, the tradition, that was all sacred business—but this? You got to be kidding me.

Finally Jim, sensing my frustration and impatience, turned off the camera and ran his hand over his face once or twice, which was, I was learning, how he mulled.

"Did you do all this for my dad?" I asked him.

"What? Booker? Oh, God, no."

"What did you do with him?"

"Well," he cleared his throat. "Well, I would let him say whatever he wanted, then afterward I would call the reporter and beg them not to print what he said. Then I would send them a case of bourbon."

"Did that work?"

"Yes, pretty much every time."

We became quiet. Jim looked out the window for a minute, then he started to put the camera away. "I'm thinking that maybe we should try that approach with you."

"Sounds like a good strategy."

"Let's get lunch."

"Sounds like an even better one."

A few days later, Booker asked me how all the training was going, so I told him about the Southern speech coach.

"They flew in a what?"

I shrugged, shook my head.

"Hell, boy, if there's one thing I know you know how to do, it's *talk.*"

I shrugged again.

"Listen," Booker said. "Don't let them tell you what to do. You be your own man. You're a god damn Beam. You say what you want, when you want."

Sounded like another plan. And I still follow that one to this day.

Another part of my education was to immerse myself in the distilling process. Know every detail, in and out. Obviously, I already knew a lot about it, I had grown up at the distillery and worked there for close to 20 years, so there weren't a whole lot of people in the world who knew more than me, but still they wanted to make sure I knew how to make bourbon blindfolded just in case I ever had to.

I had help from some of the brand people back at the corporate office, most notably a woman named Kathleen DiBenedetto. She pretty much knew everything about the Small Batches and she shared what she knew. She was a passionate lady, and she spent a lot of time teaching me the marketing ropes. But my two main teachers were Booker, the artist who intuitively knew how to make whiskey, and Dr. Jerry Dalton, our Master Distiller.

Jerry was an interesting man. He lived in the house behind us in Bardstown and had a PhD in philosophy. He had even written a book about Taoism (which, I admit, I never quite got around to reading). He was tall and big and had a mustache and, even though he was a philosopher and was soft spoken, you didn't screw with him. Among other things, he had been a Marine, and if he wanted to he could pinch your head like a grape, though I never once heard him so much as raise his voice.

Jerry was also a scientist, and his science was making bourbon. He was passionate about it. Could talk about it forever, which he did. He was as smart as they come. (I remember him breaking down some barrels, taking them apart stave by stave, then putting them back together again. He wanted to know *exactly* how a barrel was constructed. The man liked to learn.) So he put me through the paces, worked me hard. Gave me tests, made me read. Chemistry, science. Considering my lifelong allergy to school and books and teachers and homework, this was a challenge. Unlike college, though, there was no place to hide. I was in bourbon boot camp. Jerry during the day at the distillery, Booker at night at home. Man, I was getting it coming and going; they had me cornered. The only place I could relax was driving back and forth from work and home. Some days I drove as slow as I could; I didn't want to get anywhere because they were waiting for me when I did.

"No one's giving you nothing," Booker would say. "You got to earn it."

It was tough going and I'm not going to lie to you, there were times when I got tired of it all, frustrated. Why can't they just give me the job? I'm a Beam, it's my blood right.

But they made me work for it, and I kept my frustration to myself. I kept my mouth shut. I listened. I studied. In other words, for once, I made a real effort to learn. Looking back on it, they did the right thing, no question. They made me earn it. Finally, after what seemed forever, I got a passing grade from my tutors and was deemed worthy to start representing our 200-year-old brand.

"You're not going to get a second chance at this," Booker said one morning. We were sitting at the kitchen table in the Big House. (If you're thinking we spent a lot of time at our kitchen table in the Big House, you're right. Sometimes I think I've spent about 80 percent of my life at that table.) Even though he hadn't been feeling well—he was starting to get sick but we didn't know it just yet—he had made a point of getting up early to give me one more piece of advice before I headed back to the distillery to take one more quiz.

"You represent the family, everyone who works at the plant, the history. You're not some hired gun. You're a Beam. Lot of people going to be looking over your shoulder, see how you're doing, how you're acting."

"Yes, sir."

"A lot of people will be waiting for you to mess up and as soon as you do, you're back at the plant."

"I'm not going to mess up."

"Every day you got to go out there and treat it like it's the first day of a new job. Be enthusiastic. Look people in the eye. Remember people's names. Let them know you appreciate their business. Make them feel special because they are special. There's a lot of bourbons out there, they got choices. It's your job to make sure they choose ours."

"Yes, sir."

"All right then."

"All right."

I thought he was done with that morning's pep talk, but he wasn't. He had one more thing to say and this last missive, it really hit home.

"They're going to try to make you me," he said. "Don't let them. Come up with your own stories, give your own opinions, be your own man. Make them forget me."

Now I knew that wasn't ever going to happen—Booker was unforgettable—but I decided then and there that I was going to carve out my own identity, make a space for myself, do it my way.

"Yes, sir," I said, and got up to leave.

They decided to start me slow, put me in front of a few small crowds. Walk before I run. As Booker more or less said, the company was taking a risk putting me on the road in front of the public. You have to remember, in our business in particular, maybe more than most industries, image and reputation are key, and ours had been built over generations. I learned (after the fact) that there was a big debate over me back at the home office, a lot of memos flying around. There were some people who thought I could do it, but a lot of others who thought I was too country. No experience speaking in front of a crowd, of dealing with the public, of being with the media. Maybe not the right guy. He's going to say the wrong thing, or be too scared to say anything. Booker could pull it off, he was larger than life, had a personality and then some. But Fred, hell, they weren't so sure. An unknown entity. I had kept a low profile in the company, stayed in the shadows. A lot of people didn't even know I existed.

So, I admit, yeah, I was nervous. I was middle-aged, had spent most of my adult life as a working man. Now I was going to be a spokesperson. Be articulate, entertaining, informative, persuasive. Not much pressure.

I was ready enough, though. Jerry and Booker had primed me. The company and I had written a formal presentation for me. I had practiced it again and again and again, taking pains not to say "ain't" or cuss. I knew my stuff. They even bought me a new suit from Nordstrom. All systems go.

I just needed somewhere to go, and soon I was given my orders. My first-ever public appearance would be close by, at Barren River, Kentucky, for a small group of people. The group was having their annual meeting and as a little diversion, had asked that someone come down and lead them through a bourbon tasting and give a talk about the history of our company and family.

Showtime.

Jim picked me up and drove me down there. I sat in the front, went over my notes, nervous and getting more nervous. They say the two things people fear the most in life are dying and public speaking. At that point, I would have disagreed with the order of that list.

"So, what's this group?" I asked.

"What?"

"This group I'm speaking to. Who is it again? No one told me anything. I keep asking."

"Oh right, right, you should probably know that," Jim began. Remember, he was in public relations, which meant he talked a lot but never really said anything. "Well, it's interesting. A unique group, a unique opportunity."

"What are they? Rotary? Kiwanis? Bunch of doctors or lawyers or something?" A few years before, Booker had given a talk in front of a big bunch of attorneys in Philadelphia and it hadn't gone well. He had gone off on them, sent them all to hell, stormed offstage. Lawyers don't like to listen, he told me later, just talk. "Hope it's not law-yers," I said.

"No, no lawyers. It's a unique group. Not sure why they scheduled this. But it will be fun."

"Who are they?"

"Well, that part is interesting. Really interesting."

I waited. Jim cleared his throat.

"Well," he said. "It's the FBI, to be honest. The Kentucky division or something along those lines. I didn't read the whole memo."

I digested this bit of information. "What do you mean? You mean the real FBI? *The* FBI?"

"Yes, I'm pretty sure there's only one."

"You mean the guys who arrest people? The guys with guns?"

Jim cleared his throat again and switched lanes. "Well, I don't know if they'll have their guns with them. But, I mean, I guess they might, I'm not sure of their policy on firearms and alcohol, I guess I could—"

I cut him off. "Now, why the hell am I going to speak in front of a bunch of law enforcement people? You know this is a dry county we're going to, don't you? You're not even supposed to have liquor there. Plus, these guys are going be all uptight and everything."

"I don't think they'll be that uptight."

"You ever meet any FBI agents?"

"Not personally."

"They ain't Larry the Cable Guy, I can tell you that."

I was probably overreacting, but you have to remember, whiskey people and law enforcement people historically didn't get along, at least not in Kentucky. I envisioned the group, imagined those guys who used to be on the TV show *Dragnet*. Just the facts, ma'am. A ball of fun. I imagined that some of their relatives probably put some of my relatives in jail 50 years ago. Why couldn't I be speaking to a bunch of bartenders, or NFL cheerleaders? I'm being set up to fail, I thought.

Jim pulled up to the place, a small building overlooking the lake.

"I'll go park the car," he said.

"Keep it running," I said. "This won't take long."

Now I know that there are more stressful things in life then giving a speech, but you have to remember that I had never done anything like this before, so it was a big step, a milestone in my life. I remember slipping in the side door and waiting my turn to speak. The room was packed with a bunch of men in suits and ties, and they looked serious. I was following a dry speaker, I think he was talking about the FBI's new policy on reimbursement for car mileage, so at least he was an easy act to follow. But I had the jitters. Not for the first time, I wondered if I was up for this, if I was cut out to be a spokesperson, talk the talk. At the last second, I started to doubt myself, started to think I was better off back at the plant with my buds. Who was I kidding? I was a workingman, punching a clock. Now I was wearing a suit, trying to entertain and educate a roomful of complete strangers. I looked out the window. Jump in that car, push Jim out and be back in Bardstown in less than an hour. Maybe head down to the plant, help out the night shift. That's where I belonged, not here.

But when they called my name, I took a deep breath and walked up there and got it done. Spoke 45 minutes straight about the history of the family, how we make bourbon, why our products are different, better. Then we poured ourselves a little drink and tasted some of our Small Batch Bourbons. The crowd was respectful, no one pulled out any handcuffs or tried to read me my rights. It all went pretty smoothly. Not perfect, mind you. I stumbled and stuttered a few times, cussed accidentally a few times, said "ain't" probably more than I should have, but in the end I think it went okay.

"That went great," Jim said when we got back in the car.

"Went all right." I turned my head. I didn't want to let him see how much I was sweating, or hear my heart pumping like an engine piston on a wore-out truck.

Things got easier after that first tasting. My next talk was at a casino in Tunica, Mississippi, a few weeks later. A room full of high rollers—whales, they call them. The casino was trying to show their appreciation to these men, thank them for losing millions of dollars a year to them. All you can drink, all you can eat. Waitresses in short dresses. Cigar smoke. A little different from the FBI event. That's one thing I've always loved about our business: it cuts across all lines.

The casino tasting went fine. The crowd was a lot looser, and I fed off their interest and energy (and the fact that they already had a few drinks in them). I felt better up there, more confident. I remember thinking afterward that, hell, maybe I can do this.

One thing I learned about those early experiences was that preparation is everything. There's simply no substitute for being ready, practicing, rehearsing, anticipating the questions you could get. I had help starting out, good teachers, but at the end of the day, it was up to me. I was standing up there alone. So I closed my door, shut out the distractions, and got serious. I studied like I never studied before. I went over my presentation close to a hundred times, knew it backward and forward. Practiced it in front of a mirror. You might think you could get by with maybe just personality in this job, tell a few jokes, maybe a family story or two, but that will only take you so far. The people who make a mark are the people who put in the time, who take their job seriously. I learned that a little late in life, but I did learn it and I'm glad I did.

7

ROAD WARRIOR

It wasn't long before I was on the road pretty much all the time, hosting bourbon tastings, speaking at cigar smokers, fundraisers, wine and spirit trade shows, bourbon dinners, and restaurant and bar openings. When I wasn't at events, our sales team would be chauffeuring me around to retail liquor stores (we call them "off premise" locations) and to bars and restaurants ("on premise"), where I would meet and thank the people who were selling our bourbons, encouraging them to sell more. I was on the road again, just like when I was with Hank, except this time I wasn't sleeping on the floor of the tour bus, and no one was shooting out TVs. Real hotels, real beds. Real nice. *Pinocchio, you're a real boy.* New York City, Los Angeles, Seattle, San Francisco, Dallas, Phoenix, Miami, Minneapolis, Denver, Detroit, Chicago, Boston. Have bourbon, will travel.

But it wasn't a vacation. Far from it. There were ups and downs, to be sure. Sometimes an event would draw hundreds of people ready to rock 'n' roll, eager to hear what I had to say and taste some bourbon. Afterwards, they'd wait patiently in line for my autograph like I was a rock star. Other times, I would be at a bottle signing (where I sign bottles of Beam bourbon) at a roadside liquor store in the middle of nowhere and maybe three people showed. I learned early on that you had to go with the flow. Do the same job, whether it's for a packed house or one person.

And the days were long. A typical one started early, with a breakfast with our local sales team to talk about the market, hear how sales were, what's moving, what wasn't. Then it was off to see some accounts: bars, restaurants, say hello to the bartenders, the people on the front line, answer their questions. Maybe make three or four stops before noon. At lunch, it was time for a waitstaff training, where I spoke to a small group of waitresses and waiters at a top account, explained our history, how our bourbons are different, how they're made, how they should be tasted and enjoyed responsibly. Then we sampled, took a few sips. (That's usually more effective than me talking.) Next, it was more stops at retailers, mostly liquor stores, maybe do a bottle signing, then back to the hotel for a quick shower and to check my messages.

By five or six o'clock, they were back to pick me up for the evening's activities. That was usually the highlight of the day, the main reason I was in town. This could include anything from a bourbon dinner for a group of people at a large restaurant, or a bourbon tasting where I led consumers through a selection of our whiskeys. Sometimes we did something called a Great Whiskey Debate. Those were among my favorites. I would pair off with a representative of our single-malt scotch line; usually it was either Richard Paterson, a master scotch blender, or Simon Brooking, our scotch ambassador. We would make a grand entrance at these events, Richard or Simon to bagpipe music, me to a banjo, then we'd go at it, debating which is the world's preferred whiskey, scotch or bourbon. It was scripted, but after a while, we pretty much winged it, threw insults at each other—me making jokes about men in skirts, and Simon or Richard making fun of Kentucky and hillbillies. Classy, sophisticated humor. All the while we were sampling the two different types of whiskies, pointing out the differences as well as the similarities. It was part entertainment, part education, and all good fun. We used to draw hundreds of people and everyone loved it, including me. I couldn't believe I was getting paid to do it.

After the big event, it was off to dinner somewhere, usually at another top account in the area, where I got a chance to meet the manager or the owners and pose for a few pictures, maybe sign a few more bottles. Around midnight, we would hit one more bar to thank them for their patronage, then finally off to bed. That wasn't an unusual day for me. Still isn't. It was fun, but at times, it wasn't easy. I could be gone for weeks on end, living out of a suitcase.

Early on I missed my family some. I wasn't used to being away from home, from Sandy and Freddie. But Sandy knew this is what I wanted to do, knew when she married me this is what could happen, so she went along fine. Freddie handled it okay, too. He was a little older when I hit the road, so he could adapt. I think it would have been tougher on me had he been just a boy. That said, I missed my share of baseball games and birthday parties. But it was the life I had chosen. Take the good with the bad. Sacrifices, we all got to make them.

My schedule nowadays is a little easier, but not by a whole lot. I'm not as young as I used to be, so I watch what I eat and drink when I'm on the road. When I first started out, that wasn't always the case. In fact, things could get flat-out wild. Not Hank Williams, Jr. wild, but wild enough. Some of our sales boys could party as good as anyone back then. They were professionals. Adding to the situation, I think they felt an obligation to go out and show me a good time when I came to town. After a while, it became something like a competition out in the field. ("Hey, I kept Fred out to three in Chicago." "Hell, I kept him up to five in Pittsburgh.") I never had the heart to tell them that sometimes, after 16 hours of eating and drink-ing, my idea of a good time was my bed in my hotel room, but I always went along. Mornings came pretty early back then. But the sales boys were my buds, and we had some good times together, so it was worth it. In a way, the sales boys were like family. Still are.

My life on the road has given me the opportunity to meet some interesting people, celebrity types. Some of these meetings have been planned, while others have been quite accidental. Hope you don't think I'm name dropping here, but some of my experiences are worth sharing.

One such meeting occurred in Los Angeles. It was early and we had been out late the night before. No matter. When my phone went off around eight, I answered. It was a local salesman and he told me he was picking me up and that we were going to church.

"Church? It's Friday." I had made a lot of stops on the road: rodeos, barbecues, Indy car races, but church had never been on any itinerary of mine.

"Be down in the lobby in twenty," he said.

When I met him, sure enough, he took me to an empty church parking lot where a bus was waiting for me. He wouldn't tell me what the deal was, so I got on and waited. Pretty soon it began to fill up with scantily dressed, beautiful women. *This is odd*, I thought. It didn't take long for me to strike up a conversation, and I soon found out we were headed to the Playboy Mansion to have lunch with Mr. Hugh Hefner. I sat back, looked at the quiet church, wondered if I could sneak inside after all and maybe make a confession: *Forgive me, Father, for what I am about to do.*

As soon as we got to the mansion, all the women on the bus squealed with delight, took off their clothes, and jumped in the pool. Apparently they knew the drill. I had a deep desire to yell "Holy shit!" at the top of my lungs and jump up and down like Carlton Fisk did when he hit that famous home run in the World Series, but instead I played it nonchalant. I nodded my head, tried not to stare or take pictures, said "Interesting" a lot. Pretended it was just another day at the office. I did take off my sports coat, but otherwise I stayed fully clothed as I wandered around the mansion and nibbled on finger sandwiches. When I finally met Hef by the pool, I continued to play it cool. Fred Noe After Dark.

I glanced out over the water, nodded again. Two pairs of naked women were having a chicken fight, splashing each other, laughing. "You have an interesting place here," I managed to say.

He smiled and said, "Yes, I do."

Another quick story: I was in New Orleans with some of the local sales team, hanging out in a bar on Bourbon Street. It was late and I was tired and I knew I needed to get back to the hotel. You have to pace yourself in New Orleans. It's like Vegas; it's a crazy town and, if you're not careful, it can eat you alive.

"I'm going to hit the bathroom, then I'm headed back," I said, standing.

I was washing my hands at the men's room sink, when someone bumped into me from behind, kind of stumbled.

I turned around and found myself looking right into the eyes of O. J. Simpson, drunk as a skunk.

"Excuse me," he mumbled.

I nodded and finished drying my hands. The bathroom of a bar on Bourbon Street. *Hot on the trail of the real killers*, I thought.

Another memory of the early days on the road: I was back in Los Angeles doing a Great Whiskey Debate. Afterward, Chris Penn, the actor and Sean Penn's brother, came up to me and introduced himself. Turned out he was a big fan of Booker's Bourbon, loved it. We got to talking and then we decided to head out to dinner at some big-time restaurant. Some of the sales team came along and one thing led to another, and soon Chris and I got into a Booker's drinking contest. Being a professional and all, I won (I still have the twenty-dollar bill he signed), but we both lost. The next day, I had Stage Four Bust Head. That was the last time I ever got into a drinking contest with anyone, celebrity or not. I should have known better.

Other VIPs I met over the years include: Bill Murray, who was a big bourbon fan. A little-known fact: They shot the movie *Stripes* on our distillery grounds, and he used to sneak off the set and slip into Booker's office, where they would both have a private happy hour in the middle of the day. Booker had no idea who he was, couldn't have cared less, he was just happy to have someone to drink with; George Wendt (Norm!), who visited the plant from time to time, and even though he loved his beer, I personally tried to win him over to our side, and I think I succeeded; Shaquille O'Neal, who I met at a party somewhere. I took one look at him and blurted out, "You are one big son of a bitch." He looked down at me, smiled, shook my hand. "I made a lot of money being a big son of a bitch," he said.

Over the years, I got to know Robby Gordon, the great NASCAR driver. We sponsored Robby and I was thrilled. I'm a NASCAR fan, so going to his races was something special. Every so often I got to go down into the pits, watch the action up close. NASCAR is in every Southern boy's blood, so I was a kid at Christmas.

I remember one race at Charlotte Motor Speedway, they gave me a headset so I could talk to Robby from the pits. I thought he might have his mind on other matters, like driving a car at 180 miles per hour and trying not to get killed, so I didn't say much. Midway through the race, though, Robby started mumbling, complaining about some of the other drivers, the condition of his car; general griping. Before the race, his crew chief had told me that this might happen. He said that Robby sometimes got tense during a race and would let off steam while driving. It was natural, a lot of drivers do it. The crew chief also told me that if Robby went off, to tell him to just shut up and drive. So when Robby started bitching about something again, I blurted out, "Hey Robby, why don't you just shut up and drive." Robby didn't answer, didn't say a word. The crew chief, who was standing next to me, gave me kind of a surprised look, and that's when I realized he might have been kidding. But before I could say something, maybe apologize, Robby said, "Ten-four," and kept driving. He didn't say anything the rest of the race.

I also got to know another race car driver, Dan Wheldon. He was an Indy car driver, and the company sponsored him for a few years. We hung out before and after races and we became pretty good friends. I like to think that I played a role in his winning the Indy 500 back in 2005. That year, I had read that the owner of the horse that won the 2005 Kentucky Derby had bought a $100 ticket to win on his horse, gave it to his jockey, and told him to put it in his shoe. I thought that was inspiring. So I went out and got a $100 ticket to win for the Indy 500, gave it to Dan, and told him to put it his shoe while he was driving the big race.

"Don't ask questions," I said. He didn't, and like I said, he went out and won.

We became good friends after that. I always looked forward to watching his races, whether it was in person or on TV. Unfortunately, I was watching from my living room when he crashed and died in 2011 during the last race of the circuit in Las Vegas. Like everyone else, I was stunned and saddened by that tragedy, and to see it before my very eyes, to see a friend die like that, was something I'll never forget. A helpless, dark feeling. He was a great driver, but more importantly, a decent man. He died doing what he loved, but that's little consolation. The whole racing world misses him to this day.

In addition to race car drivers, I've also been lucky to get know some people in the music business. I love all kinds of music, but obviously country is my favorite because it's part of the culture and fabric of Kentucky; it's pretty much all we listen to. A lot of the biggest country stars have come from my home state. There's a highway in eastern Kentucky, Highway 23, that's officially known as the Country Music Highway because so many big stars were born and raised near it. People like Loretta Lynn, Naomi and Judd, Dwight Yoakam, Patty Loveless, Ricky Skaggs, Billy Ray Cyrus, and more all grew up in close range to that road. So I grew up listening to and loving county music. It's a passion of mine and it keeps me company when I'm alone in hotel rooms or on those long international flights. I've been especially happy to get to know the duo of Eddie Montgomery and Troy Gentry. They're Kentucky boys who made good by making great music. I've gotten to know Kid Rock, too. Like Eddie and Troy, he's been sponsored by the company, and over the years I've had a chance to spend some quality time with him. And like Eddie and Troy, he's a good guy, straightforward and real and a pleasure to be with. Though he's not really country, I like his music too.

One thing I've learned through my days on the road and from all of the people I have met is that whether you're a celebrity or a brand-new bartender, everyone has something to offer, everyone has a story to share. Doesn't matter what they're talking about—their jobs, a memory, an opinion—I try to hear what people are saying. I try to listen and maybe learn something. Funny, for the first half of my life, I wasn't much of student; didn't put much stock in what people had to tell me, had no patience for learning new things. Now it seems I can't get enough. I regret not shutting my mouth and listening when I was younger. But I'm glad I'm doing it now. The world's a classroom; took me too long to realize that.

BOURBON PRIMER

What Is Whiskey?

I've talked a lot about bourbon, but I thought I could take a minute and maybe talk about other whiskies or distilled spirits too. For the record, Beam makes more than just bourbon. In fact, we make more than 80 brands: scotches, tequilas, Irish whiskey, Canadian whisky, liqueurs, mixes, and ready-to-drink cocktails like Skinnygirl Margaritas. We pretty much got it all.

Now, *whiskey* is defined is a spirituous liquor made from grains. As I've said, bourbon is a whiskey, but not all whiskies are bourbon. Bourbon's main grain is corn. Number-two yellow corn. I've already gone over the exact definition of it; now I'll run through some other definitions as well. (Please note: some of these spirits, like vodka and tequila, technically aren't whiskies since they aren't made from grains.)

Scotch: Good stuff. Main ingredient is malted barley. It's made in Scotland and has been for centuries. (The first mention of this is in some document dated 1495, so the

(continued)

(*continued*)

stuff is old). It's aged in oak barrels for at least three years and bottled at a minimum of 80 proof (which means it's 40 percent alcohol). A single-malt whiskey means it is entirely produced from malt in one distillery. Blended scotch whiskey is blended together with scotch from other distilleries, with neutral grain spirits added.

We have some great scotches, including Laphroaig, which comes from Islay, a small island off of Scotland.

Canadian Whisky: A relative of our bourbon, this is a whisky (they don't use the "e" when they spell it; not sure whye) that must be made in Canada. A lot of people think you have to use all rye in the recipe, but that's not the case. It's made from other grains (especially corn) that are blended together. Canadian whisky is typically lighter and smoother than other whiskies, has to be bottled at 80 proof minimum, and aged at least three years in oak barrels.

We sell the best Canadian Whisky out there: Canadian Club. I'm sure you've heard of it.

Irish Whiskey: Short definition: whiskey that's made in Ireland from a fermented mash of cereal grains. Unlike bourbon, most Irish whiskies are distilled three times and typically bottled at anywhere from 80 to all the way up to 115 proof and aged in used bourbon barrels.

Our portfolio of brands includes four Irish whiskies from the Cooley Distillery: Kilbeggan®, Greenore®, Tyrconnell®, and Connemara®. They're all good.

Tennessee Whiskey: This whiskey is similar to bourbon, but there is a difference: they use something called the Lincoln County Process to add some flavor to the liquor. That process involves filtering or "leaching" the whiskey through a layer of maple charcoal before its aged. This gives this whiskey a smoky nose and smell, and since they are adding a flavor, by law they cannot call themselves a bourbon. We don't make any of this stuff.

In addition to whiskies, we also make the following spirits. Technically they're not all really whiskies, because some of them are made from other things like fruits and vegetables, not grains like bourbon and scotch.

Tequila: Mostly made in the Mexican state of Jalisco, this spirit comes from the blue agave plant that grows in the region. Bottled at about 80 to 110 proof (40 to 55 percent alcohol), the aging process ranges from unaged (*blanco* or *plata*), to *reposado* (aged 2 to 11 months), and *añejo* (aged at least one year). Extra *añejo* is aged more than three years. The aged tequila is the fancy stuff and is compared to cognac, a worthy comparison.

Our portfolio of tequilas includes the Sauza® brands and El Tesoro.

Vodka: I drank a lot of this in Mother Russia. In the old days, it was primarily colorless and flavorless, and is composed of water and the distillation of fermented things like grains, fruits, or even potatoes. Mostly bottled at anywhere from 40 percent to 80 percent proof, it's made in a lot of countries, including Russia, Poland, Hungary, Sweden, Lithuania, and other Eastern and Central European locations. As I mentioned, vodka used to be flavorless, but that has changed; now it comes in a variety of flavors, and we have all kinds. Great straight up with ice, or as part of a cocktail, vodka is a spirit that makes the world go 'round.

Beam sells a number of vodkas, including Pinnacle® Vodka, Pucker™ Flavored Vodka, Skinnygirl™ Vodka with natural flavors, EFFEN® Vodka, VOX® Vodka, Kamchatka® Vodka, Wolfschmidt® Vodka, and Gilbey's® Vodka.

(*continued*)

(continued)

Rum: One of the oldest spirits and still one of earth's best selling. It's primarily made from sugarcane products like molasses or cane juice. Most rum comes the Caribbean and Latin America, but some can come all the way from Australia and New Zealand. Proofs and aging requirements vary, depending on the country it's made in, so I won't list any of those here.

Our rums include Cruzan®, Calico Jack®, Ronrico®, and Gilbey's®.

Liqueur and Cordials: These are typically schnapps or brandies and are sweet, flavor-infused spirits. They aren't aged very long and really can be made and distilled from a variety of things, like grains, potatoes and molasses. A wide range of flavors can then be added once they come off the still.

We make one of the most successful lines of liqueurs, DeKuyper®, which has close to 60 different flavors, from Peachtree to Buttershots.

8

THE WORLD ISN'T
AS BIG AS I THOUGHT

About a year into my job of being Bourbon Ambassador and traveling the county, I got a new assignment: go overseas. Mr. Intercontinental. This was a big deal for me. Up until then, the closest I had been to foreign travel was Canada, and, let's face it, that's not all that foreign. Other than the fact that they spell whisky without an "e" and like hockey more than basketball, Canadians look, act, and talk pretty much like Americans. (Or we talk like them, depending on your perspective.)

Fortunately for me, my first trip was to London, where, like Canada, they speak English pretty well, which makes sense considering they invented it. So I packed up and headed out there for a few days and hosted a bourbon dinner with an up-and-coming chef named Jamie Oliver. He would later go on to big things as the Naked Chef, though he was fully clothed when we worked together.

I remember strolling along the River Thames while I was in London, seeing Parliament (the biggest building I've ever seen), then Buckingham Palace (where I saw the changing of the guard), Big Ben, and statues of Winston Churchill (who looked like a big bulldog.) I tried to take it all in, eyes wide open. I knew this was a unique experience, being there to represent my family and our bourbons, and I wanted to appreciate it.

My eyes got a lot wider on my next trip a short while later. Destination: Russia. Now, you have to remember that I am a child of the Cold War. I remembered air raid drills, hiding under my desk, forehead pressed against my knees while some siren wailed, so I had some misgivings about the trip. This wasn't Canada, this wasn't London. Different place. Whole other world.

I knew that right away when I landed in Saint Petersburg and saw a line of old, gray military aircraft on the runway, the red star bright on their tails. When I got off the plane, snow was swirling around on the tarmac, and I thought I was in a James Bond movie, or maybe a documentary about World War II, as though some jeep was waiting to whisk me off to an underground bunker where I would review the latest troop movements.

Inside the airport I saw soldiers, machine guns at their side, faces as cold and hard as a January morning. It didn't take me long to get lost; my contact, the local sales rep, was late, so I ended up wandering around by myself, thinking, "Toto, we're not in Kentucky anymore."

My local guy finally showed (I don't think I was ever so happy to see a liquor salesman in my life) and we were off. Driving through the streets of Saint Petersburg, I got a sense of two sets of history: great, old domed buildings, relics from the time of the czars I guess, sprinkled in with lots of gray, old, nondescript ones from the Communist era.

The food was good, though. I tend to judge a country on their cuisine and how close it is to Kentucky food, and it surprisingly passed the test: a lot of meat and potatoes. And I had a lot, and I mean *a lot* of vodka. Seems everywhere I went, someone was putting a glass under my nose, asking me what I thought. Just like 100 years ago in Kentucky, there's a lot of home distillers in Russia, everyone has their own special recipe. I admired their craftsmanship, though I can't say I enjoyed their spirits that much: I am a brown-liquor man, through and through.

Most of the countries I visited tend to blur together—that's the downside of high-speed travel—but that Russia trip stands out because it was such a foreign place, so completely different than anything I could imagine. Even though it's been more than 10 years since that first trip, I remember it pretty well.

I especially remember one of our last nights. We were in Moscow now, a bigger version of Saint Pete's, and I had just conducted a long day of media interviews. The articles would appear in the Russian papers and magazines after I was long gone. I thought that was odd. Usually when I get somewhere, I do my press interviews as soon as I arrive, so people know I'm in town and where I'm going to be. I remember asking my contact about that.

"It's safer this way," he said.

"What do you mean, safer?"

"It's too dangerous to have the articles run while you're still here. Too many people would read them, learn you were here, maybe find out where you were staying."

I still didn't understand. "Isn't that the whole point?"

Finally he said, "Kidnappers. They would love to get someone like you."

"Why?"

"Ransom."

"Oh." I thought about that. "They'd be wasting their time with me. Nobody's going to pay to get me back."

Regardless, I was pretty careful for the rest of the day, looking over my shoulder, wondering if I was being followed, checking to see where the exits where. But by the time night came, I was over it and ready to relax. Hell, Russia's no more dangerous than New York. So the local team and I decided to go to a big nightclub, owned ironically enough by an American who had invited us to stop by. It wasn't part of our official itinerary, but my group thought it would be polite to stop in and have a quick drink. Apparently the owner was very influential in Moscow.

When we got to the place, we looked around and agreed it was a nice enough place. It reminded me of a casino in Las Vegas: loud music, disco lights, and beautiful women. I mean eye-popping, model beautiful. (Sandy, don't you read this next part.)

I was leaning over the bar, ordering my Beam straight up with water back, when one of the women, maybe the most beautiful in the entire place, came over and tried to engage me in conversation.

"Where from?" she asked.

I was hoping she was a kidnapper. "Kentucky," I said.

This got no reaction, so I tried again. "United States of America. USA. Ever hear of it?"

Apparently she had. She shot me a dazzling smile, then said, "You want sex?"

I didn't think I had heard her exactly right. Then I thought maybe "sex" meant something else in Russian, like cigar or vodka or cheeseburger, so I said, "No, I just ordered bourbon. Jim Beam, but thank you."

"Want sex?"

The second time clarified her offer. *Man, they don't waste time in Russia*, I thought. In Kentucky, you have to buy a girl a few drinks first, maybe dinner, to even have a chance. "No, but thank you for asking," I said. "Mighty kind of you."

She drifted away, but a few minutes later, another woman, equally attractive, approached me. I nodded hello and sipped at my drink.

"Want sex?" she asked.

Man, she made the other one seem shy. I sniffed myself. *It must be my cologne*, I thought.

"I think I'm okay on that front," I said, and walked away.

A little later, someone from my group came over and told me to drink up, we're going. We weren't in a bar, he said. Apparently we were in one of the biggest brothels in Moscow. Like I said, different world.

I made a return trip to Russia, or at least tried to, a few years later. I was a seasoned traveler by then, had been about everywhere, but hadn't been back to Russia since my first trip. I wasn't scared this time. Mostly I was tired. I had been on the road for a few weeks, touring Europe, and I was ready to go home.

I flew in from Warsaw and when I got to the airport in Moscow, I went through customs half asleep. By then, I knew the drill, knew what to do and say. But when I got up to the main desk and handed them my visa, rather than the rubber stamp I was expecting, I got a scowl and a question.

"Where visa?"

I pointed to what I had just given him. "Right here."

"No visa!" he said.

"Yes visa," I said.

"No visa." He handed me back what I thought was my visa.

I shrugged, started to get a little nervous. "Well, let me clear this up." I pulled out my phone and tried to call Linda Hayes back in Clermont. Linda made all my travel arrangements. If anyone could get me out of this, she could.

"No phone!" the customs man said. He was very large and reminded me of someone from one of those James Bond movies.

I almost said, "Yes phone," but caught myself. Then I swallowed. Some other guards, I noticed, were staring at me. At that point, I missed Bardstown, Kentucky, more than I ever had in my life.

"I need to make a call," I said.

Apparently this was the wrong thing to say. The customs man snapped his finger, and two guards came over and escorted me off.

I ended up in the far end of the airport in a small room with a naked light bulb hanging from a wire. *Name, rank, and serial number, that's all I'm giving them*, I thought. That and *maybe* the exact number and location of our rack houses.

The two guards glared at me and I kept nodding my head and smiling, wondering if any members of SEAL Team Six were in the neighborhood. After a while, they asked me a few questions in Russian, and I just nodded my head in American. We were at an impasse. Finally they left, and I saw my chance. I slipped out my phone and was about to try and call Linda again, when the head guard, the one who greeted me at customs, came back in and caught me in the act of apparent espionage. He yelled at me, grabbed my phone, and stormed off.

A minute later, a woman came in and told me in broken English that I didn't have a proper visa and that I should have never been allowed off the airplane. She then said I needed to pay a fine.

"How much?" I was hoping for something in the vicinity of a speeding ticket.

"Two thousand rubles," she said.

I was a little light in the ruble department, so I asked if she took credit cards.

"No."

"How about traveler's checks? I got a lot of them."

"No."

"American dollars? I can probably get that somehow."

"No."

I thought for a while. "How about some bourbon? I'll set you up for life. You can open your own liquor store when I'm done with you."

"No. Rubles!" She left in a huff.

I was wondering what Siberia was like that time of year, when the two guards came back and took me under the arm, then hustled me out of the room, back outside, and onto the tarmac, where my plane, the one I had just gotten off, was waiting. They pointed to my luggage, handed my phone to the flight attendant and told them not to give it back to me until I was in Poland. Then they curtly nodded goodbye. I got on that plane as fast as I could, ordered a drink, and didn't relax until snow-covered Moscow was just a dot over my shoulder.

I haven't been back to Mother Russia since, but next time I do, I plan on bringing the right visa *and* 2,000 rubles, just to play it safe.

Now, I don't want to give you all the wrong impression of Russia. Overall, despite my initial misgivings, I liked the country and I enjoyed my visit. The people are hardworking, straightforward and couldn't have been more decent. They've had some tough times over there, daily life is still a struggle for some, but they're working hard to change things, make things better. As soon as I got there, my experience at the airport notwithstanding, I learned that they liked Americans and liked working with us. They also like our whiskey, which shows they are a nation of great taste and style.

I've been to other places: Japan, where I was something of a spectacle (they kept taking pictures of me; I think they thought I was Godzilla or something); Australia and New Zealand, where the party never, ever stopped (they like their good times Down Under, especially Jim Beam & Cola, a premixed cocktail that's sold in bottles and cans); Hungary, where I had breakfast overlooking the Danube, a pretty river that reminded me of the Ohio; and Dubai, where everything is under construction, cranes as far as you can see.

An odd thing happened to me in Dubai. I was on my way to a meeting with two women, sales associates for the region, and when I tried to open the door to let them into the hotel, they quickly told me to close it.

"What?"

"Please close it as soon as you can. Please!" They nervously looked around.

I closed the door.

"Don't ever hold a door open for us again," they said.

"You say so."

Later on they explained that public displays of affection toward women were against the law. I guess holding open a door for a woman came under that heading, so I never did it again. Hell, in certain states back in America, you can't buy or sell liquor on Sundays, so I guess everyone's got their own peculiar laws.

I was even in the Czech Republic; it's a big importer of our Jim Beam Bourbon. Prague is a beautiful city, unlike any other I had ever been to before. I felt like I had fallen back in time as I strolled the streets. A real, old-world charm to everything. And I loved the food. They eat a lot of pork over there and I'm a big fan of the other white meat. What I remember most about my trip is a little incident I had with the local sales gal. She made the mistake of trying to impress me by drinking bourbon at dinner like it was Gatorade and she had just finished the Boston Marathon. I felt sorry for her; she was new to our whiskey, probably felt obligated to guzzle it in front of me ("It is so very good, Mr. Noe!"), and she paid a big price. I kept telling her to slow down, but once you're on the slippery slope, you tend to pick up speed going down Bourbon Mountain. I know, I've been there a few times. The next morning, she was supposed to pick me up early and spend the day with me, take me around sightseeing, but she never showed. I feared the worst, but late in the afternoon, she called and told me she wasn't feeling well. "I think I caught something," she said.

"I think what you caught is a form of the Bust Head," I said.

"Bust What?"

"It's an affliction common to new bourbon drinkers. I'll see you tomorrow, honey. Drink plenty of water and keep the curtains drawn tight. You'll be as good as new tomorrow."

The next day, when we were at a big meeting, the woman's boss asked how the sightseeing had gone the day before. The woman shot me a pleading look, but I already knew what I was going to say.

"Great. She was the perfect tour guide."

I figured that white lie would make me a friend for life, and I was right. We still stay in touch.

I've made other friends for life. Everywhere I go, no matter the country, people are friendly, warm, and engaging. They're curious too. They want to learn about our whiskies, our family, the USA. The more countries I visit, the more similarities I see in cultures. No matter where we live, we have a lot in common.

When I first started traveling, I thought the world was a big place. I admit, I was a little intimidated, overwhelmed maybe (I thought Bowling Green was a big city) but now I see things in a different light. The food may be different, the customs, the clothes, but in the end, people are people.

Bourbon helps. It's a common language, everyone understands it, no matter where they're from. A drink or two can put people at ease, bring them together, open them up. Sometimes I think the whole world is like one big bar, and I'm the world's bartender. Making friends, keeping them. It's like being back at Toddy's, except this time I don't have any angry wives coming after me.

BOURBON PRIMER

A Global Spirit

While bourbon got its start in the United States (as I've said, it's America's Native Spirit), it's enjoyed the world over now. Jim Beam Bourbon is distributed in nearly 100 countries, and we sell millions of cases overseas every year. Those are big numbers, and they'll most likely continue to grow over time. One thing my world travels have shown and taught me is that people have a taste for our whiskey, can't seem to get enough of it. I still get a little charge every time I walk into a club or restaurant in some faraway place like Tokyo, or Budapest, or the Canary Islands off the coast of Africa and see our bourbon prominently displayed on the back bar. A little piece of America, a big piece of my family. Sometimes I wonder what the ghosts are thinking. Something along the lines of, "We've come a long way from Hardin Creek," I imagine.

Listed below are the countries that import the most Jim Beam Bourbon.

- Australia
- New Zealand
- Germany
- United Kingdom
- Hungary
- Canada
- The Czech Republic
- Japan

9

BOURBON AND CHANGE

A lot of people ask me where the bourbon industry is headed. And to help answer that question, I think it would be smart to take a look at where it has been.

Now, I touched on some history in the first chapter, but kind of stopped right after Prohibition. I'd like to pick it up from there, if you don't mind.

As I said, bourbon took a big hit from Prohibition—it could have been the death penalty for us. But we picked ourselves up and, slowly and surely, put things back together and started producing quality, one-of-a-kind whiskey again. It took some time, about a year and a half, to get things running, but in March 1935, we completed our first run of whiskey and threw a party at the distillery to celebrate.

When my great-grandfather died, my Uncle Jere was already running things so the transition was smooth and that helped us move forward. Uncle Jere wasn't really a distiller. Though he obviously knew the process backward and forward, he was more of a promoter and salesman—a marketer, though they didn't use that word a lot back then. He really got us going again, opened up channels of distribution, marketed the heck out of the brand. Even though we had other bourbon brands like Old Tub and something called Cave Hollow (not sure who did the product naming back then), for all practical purposes, we were a one-trick pony at that time and that pony was Colonel James B. Beam Bourbon, which soon became simply Jim Beam Bourbon. For a long time, that was enough. It was a great product, still is, and America gradually agreed. Soon it was flying off the shelves, recording double-digit growth, and this helped lift the entire bourbon industry. From about 1950 to 1966, sales of the category grew and grew and eventually bourbon became the number one whiskey in the nation.

During that time, the company also began shipping more and more bourbon overseas. Seems during World War II, American GIs had been passing the bottle around to their English and French counterparts, to name a few. Sharing the American spirit. The seeds had been successfully planted, and those seeds took root. That helped our sales even more and soon we had to expand, add another distillery (hence the plant in Boston, Kentucky, Booker's private laboratory.)

We rode the Jim Beam Bourbon horse hard, rode it as long as we could, rode it far and wide. But soon enough that horse got tired and started to get passed up. By the 1970s people were starting to look for other beverage options, and bourbon began losing ground to other spirits. The decline was slow at first, but eventually it picked up steam and soon it was undeniable; after a good 20-year stretch, we were heading in the wrong direction. Bourbon was old fashioned; been there, done that. Even the names of most of the brands reflected the position of the industry: Old Taylor, Old Fitzgerald, Old Charter. Everything about bourbon was old. Especially our customers.

What exacerbated the situation was what happened to Old Crow. For a time in the early seventies, it was a big brand, bigger than ours. Then something happened to the product. Conflicting stories on what, exactly. One story has it that they deliberately monkeyed with the recipe, watered it down some to make it go further so they could keep up with the demand. Another version has them losing the original recipe, which I admit sounds a little farfetched. (There's only one copy of the recipe? No one has it memorized?) Anyway, it wasn't the same bourbon; people noticed, stopped buying it, and when it went south it took a part of the category down with it.*

*The recipe situation was eventually rectified. We bought Old Crow in the 1980s, and it's a good product now. Don't believe me? Go taste it. Good everyday whiskey.

By the 1980s beer and wine (and their cousins, wine coolers; remember Bartles & Jaymes?) were riding high, and then along came vodka, and finally scotch and the single malts. Big change in the wind. Suddenly you haven't made it unless you're seen holding onto a glass of Scotland's finest, nosing its peaty aroma, or asking for a martini, shaken not stirred, extra dry, with two olives. Not many people were asking for Beam, straight up, and the ones who did probably personally knew my great-grandfather.

So it was time to innovate, get creative, rewrite the book. That's easier said than done, of course. It's never easy revising the game plan, especially one you've been following for about 200 years. But as I've mentioned, Booker, my dad, did it. To be fair, he wasn't the only one in the industry to do it, there were others for sure, but Booker made the biggest splash with his own special bourbon, Booker's, and in the process created the Small Batch Bourbons.

As I've mentioned, the Small Batch Bourbons—Booker's, Knob Creek, Basil Hayden's, and Baker's—helped kick-start things, let people know that we were still around. They proved to everyone that we could keep up, be relevant. The most important people we proved that to was ourselves. Hey, we can change after all. Look at us, man! We're good.

So Small Batch marked an evolutionary milestone for us. Sales were strong. Bourbon was back and growing, and starting in the late nineties, a real renaissance took place.

But instead of following that success up, you know what we did?

Hell, not much.

From the early nineties, when Small Batch was launched, until just a few years ago, there really wasn't much in the way of innovation in the bourbon industry. As I just said, sales were solid, especially for Knob Creek, and that was good enough. All the different distilleries had their own version of Small Batch, so we were all doing okay, but . . .

There's an expression I've heard in the accounting industry, "Things go bad before they go bad." This means that while things might be fine for now, if you look down the road, the numbers are telling you they might not be as fine in a few years. I'm not saying that things were going to go bad in our industry, there's no way you could predict that, but one thing I do know is that rather than wait for a storm to hit like we did back in the Old Seventies, we did something about it.

We got creative, did a little innovating.

Enter Red Stag by Jim Beam, the very first flavor-infused bourbon in our long, long history. Black cherry flavor to be exact. (Check out page 70 for its taste profile.) This marked a big change for us, and the category shook things up. To be honest, there were a lot of skeptics out there, and probably the biggest one of all was me. I admit when we launched the product a few years ago, I pitched a holy fit. I didn't like the idea of flavoring bourbon at all, and I let my opinions be known. People in the industry knew what I liked to drink: Beam, straight up, maybe some water back. I'm a purist, classically trained, studied at the Juilliard of whiskey. Adding a flavor to the centuries-old recipe? Sacrilege and holy shit! What would the ghosts think? Booker will come back and start kicking ass. I didn't even want to taste the product. But the brand people worked hard on me, flew down to see me, kept after me to try it. So eventually, I took a sip. Then I took another, and then one more and before you know it, it was all gone. Not bad. In fact, more than not bad; pretty good. Booker might even approve. I cleared my throat, looked at my empty glass. Need to play politician here, clarify my original position. Now, what I meant to say was. . . .

Red Stag by Jim Beam was a hit, took off a like a Kid Rock song going up the charts. (Red Stag by Jim Beam sponsored him, in case you're confused by my reference.) This was what they call a watershed moment, a turning point for Beam Inc.

The product was important to us in a lot of ways: (1) We changed before *we had to*. We went out to market with something new, something different on our own, not in response to some problem or shrinking market. (2) We reached out to a whole new audience, people who might not necessarily be bourbon drinkers, such as women. (3) We broadened the shoulders of our flagship brand, Jim Beam Bourbon. People who liked Red Stag by Jim Beam might tiptoe over to the big dog, pet it, take it for a walk around the block, come back the next day, become friends. So it was all good. In fact, it was so good, that we added two more flavors: Honey Tea and Spice. More variety for more people to choose from. More flavors for bartenders to play with. A centuries-old category and a centuries-old company, getting all creative. Look at us now, brother.

But we didn't stop there. Not this time. This time we understood that the consumer likes new things, like to see what's out there. So in 2011, we came out with another new expression: Devil's Cut. Killer name. Killer bourbon. This one's got a pretty good backstory and I'm proud to say that I'm in it.

Years ago, back when I was maybe around 13, Booker was fooling around at the distillery, trying to make some wine, and he needed a barrel to age in it.

"Drive up to the dump room and get me an old barrel, hurry up," he said, throwing me the keys to his truck. I was amazed, not that he was making wine at a bourbon distillery—Booker made everything at the distillery—but that he had just given me the keys to his truck. Like I said, I was 13. So I ran over to that truck before he could change his mind, threw it in gear, drove up to the dump room, and asked one of the workers to help me load a barrel into the back.

"You know, there's a lot of good whiskey in that barrel," he said after we were done.

I looked at that man. He was an old-timer, a whiskey veteran through and through, and I thought he had probably drank his lunch. That barrel was as empty as my pocket.

"There's nothing in it," I said.

"Hell, boy, look close, get your head in there."

I didn't budge. In fact, I started inching away, backwards. "Don't see nothing."

"Can't see it with your eyes, you have to see it with your nose! There's whiskey in there all right and a lot of it. It's in that wood, Freddie. It's hiding in there deep. The wood absorbs it and it stays there getting old and good. Got the best flavor. Can't you smell it?"

I closed my eyes, took a sniff, got a good whiff. "Oh." Suddenly I understood. Kind of.

"I'm going to give you another barrel, Freddie. Take it on home and put some water in it, put the bung back on it, roll it around for a while, sweat it, then set it upside down on a couple of bricks. Remember to put a pan under it. In a day or so, knock that bung out of it and you're going to get a pan full of high quality bourbon."

I studied that empty barrel. No bourbon, then bourbon. Just add water. This sounded like magic. "You sure about that?"

He rolled another barrel over to the truck and lifted it on in. "Hell, yes, I'm sure about that. Now go home and try it. You'll thank me one day." He started back to the dump floor but stopped halfway and turned. "Hey, how old are you now?"

"I just turned twenty-one."

"Right. You and me both, boy. Listen, just to play it safe, don't go telling your dad I told you this now. Tell him one of your cousins told you, Baker maybe, or you learned about this at school or something."

"Yes, sir, I won't," I said, eyes still on those empty barrels.

So I went home with that extra barrel and did what the old-timer said: put water in it, sweated it, then set it up behind the shed in the corner of our backyard away from prying eyes. That first night I checked on it, stared at that barrel for a long time, said the Rosary, praying for the second coming of bourbon. A couple of days later, when I knocked the bung out, my prayers were answered: drinking whiskey flowed out of that once-empty barrel; that pan became full of it.

Fast forward about 40 years. I'm sitting in a meeting with our innovation team, kicking around ideas, looking for the next big thing. Someone asked me about growing up at the plant, what Booker did when he was at Boston, and that story came back to me, so I shared it. Wish I had sunglasses after I did, because so many light bulbs went off, I almost went blind.

Devil's Cut was a hit. (See its taste profile on page 70.) A great-tasting whiskey that's a little different. Wish I could remember that old-timer's name. I'd give him a case (or two) for sure.

Devil's Cut, Red Stag by Jim Beam—we keep moving forward. Not long ago we came out with a Knob Creek Single Barrel, in addition to the best-selling Small Batch version, and a Knob Creek Rye. More variety, more innovation, more choices for our customers; something new from a very old company. All good stuff.

And our sales have responded to what we're doing. Thanks to our innovation and our premiumization (upscale brands), bourbon was the fastest-growing large category in the United States in 2011. That's something the whole industry is proud of, something we can all brag on.

So, it's working . . . and we keep working, no longer content to rest on our laurels. What's next, I'm not sure. (Hell, I wouldn't tell you if I knew anyway.) I imagine new flavors, new ways to finish our bourbons, maybe higher-end products, maybe not. We'll have successes and we'll probably have a few belly flops too. All I can be sure of is that whatever we finally come up with will be different and, hopefully, good.

I also know that any new products will remain true to our core values and our history. In other words, our integrity and our long tradition and sacred process will be protected. I'm going to make sure of that. I'm a Beam, and that's my job.

BOURBON PRIMER

The Beam Master Distillers and Their Bourbons

Over the generations, my forefathers have overseen the production of a number of various bourbons. Here's a partial list of some of the bigger brands and who oversaw what during their entry into the marketplace. This list is not all-inclusive; we produced a number of small bourbons back in the old days.

Jacob Beam and David Beam (unofficial name):
   o   Old Jake Beam

David M. Beam:
   o   Old Tub™

Jim Beam (pre-Prohibition):
   o   Clear Springs Bourbon
   o   Pebbleford

Jim Beam (post-Prohibition):
   o   F.G. Walker, Five Beams, Cave Hollow, and Colonel James B. Beam
   o   Jim Beam® Bourbon

T. Jeremiah Beam:
   o   Jim Beam® Rye
   o   Beam's Pin Bottle (8 and 10 years old)
   o   Beam's Choice
   o   Jim Beam Black® Label

Booker Noe:
   o   Distiller's Masterpiece by Jim Beam**
   o   Jim Beam Black™

(continued)

(*continued*)

- o   Jim Beam Ready-to-Drink (and Cola/Ginger Ale)
- o   Booker's®, Baker's®, Basil Hayden's®, Knob Creek®

Fred Noe:

- o   Jim Beam® 1795*
- o   Jim Beam® Small Batch*
- o   Knob Creek® Single Barrel
- o   Knob Creek® Rye
- o   Red Stag by Jim Beam®
- o   Devil's Cut®
- o   Jim Beam® Honey*

---

*Limited edition
**International only

10

THE BEAM WAY

HOW TO BUILD A COMPANY
THAT LASTS

Back in 2011, Jim Beam Brands went public. I had the privilege of going to the floor of the New York Stock Exchange with our CEO, Matt Shattock, and other executives to celebrate. We also changed our name to Beam Inc. that day. Pretty simple, pretty straightforward. One word that says it all.

As you can imagine, it was a proud day for us and it got me thinking. As I've said two or three hundred times in this book, we're an old company, one of the oldest in

America. Not many companies have a history like ours. Long, consistent. Not many companies have had one family involved from the start.

So, as I said, I did a little thinking about the reason for our longevity, pondered why we've outlasted dozens of competitors—hell, dozens of industries (the horse and buggy, the telegraph, eight-tracks, VCRs)—and in the process, I put together a short list of things that have contributed to our success. If you're already working in a company or thinking of building one that lasts, you may want to read up. (Look at me now: bad student turned teacher.) Most of these observations and thoughts are pretty basic, really more common sense than anything. You probably won't find many of them in a management course at Harvard. But that's how we like to operate at Beam. Direct. To the point. I think that approach works best for most things in business and in life, so here it goes, What Fred Noe Knows:

1. *Discipline and focus:* I think I'll start here because when you talk about my family, you have to talk about focus. Throughout the years, we've maintained a single-mindedness about us that has kept us on the right track. From the start, when Jacob carted that pot still over the Wilderness Road into Kentucky and set up shop, he knew what he wanted to do and he stuck with it. Eyes on the prize. I'm sure he got sidetracked from time to time, I'm sure obstacles arose

and unforeseen challenges surfaced, but regardless, he stayed true to the task at hand, and never lost sight of the goal: make the best whiskey.

I think focus—setting one goal and never deviating from it, having it serve as your guiding light through good times and bad—is more than just important for a company and for a brand, it's essential. Everything you do has to relate back to it. So make sure you have a goal, just one now, and go out after it. And every day, make sure you're making progress toward it. At the end of the day, when you're turning out the lights, ask yourself: Did we move a little closer to it? Did we get anything done today that we didn't yesterday? And it's important to remember not to get discouraged. Progress comes slow but then it can come fast. It took us generations to get to where we are now. So keep your focus and don't get distracted. Success doesn't come overnight. If you do something long enough like we have, eventually, you'll reach that goal. Then it's time to set a new one.

2. *Innovation:* I kind of covered this in the last chapter, but it's so important that I'll add to it. No matter what business you're in, change is critical. I've seen this close up. After years and years—hell, after generations really—the distilling industry is changing. There's lots of small microdistilleries popping up around the country making all kinds of new, different, and in some cases even good whiskey and spirits.

They're even making bourbon in New York. The next Jim Beam might be out there for all I know. My point is that you've not only got to keep up, you have to anticipate what's coming down the pike. Keep your eyes and ears open to new opportunity, keep your mouth shut, and take good notes. Listen and learn. I already told you what happened to the bourbon industry in the 1970s: we got caught flat-footed, put our head in the sand, and when things started to change, we weren't ready. It showed on our bottom line, and we ended up paying a steep price.

We've learned our lesson since, though, and we're into innovating now. Research and development. Red Stag and Devil's Cut are proof positive that we're committed to new thinking. In fact, we're so committed to it that we built a state-of-the-art Global Innovation Center on the grounds of the Clermont distillery. This is where science and craft meet. This is where good ideas come from, ideas that are going to make a difference in our future and in our industry. So always be thinking about what's next. I guarantee you, your competitors are.

One more thing in regards to innovation: don't be afraid to fail while you're trying to get creative and launch something new. Over the years, we've made mistakes; all our products haven't been home runs. Years ago, we came out with a tequila that had chiles in it. A novelty. This was going to change the game, make us a player in the category. Well, that product bombed like the New Coke, and it's just a memory now. We've had other strikeouts too—a micro-bourbon (never was sure what that was) that had micro-sales comes to mind. Regardless, we kept plugging away. So don't be discouraged; get off the ground, dust yourself off, and keep looking for the next best thing. After more than 200 years, we still are.

3. *Humility and remembering your roots:* Keep it real, brother. Never get too impressed with your own success. Never think you know all the answers, can solve all the problems. Never think you can't get better. Most importantly, remember where you came from. Remember your roots. I think that's something we've done pretty well at Beam over the generations. It started with our family; overall we're a pretty modest bunch. Jim Beam was a reserved man, and for the most part my uncles and cousins were and are a pretty laid-back bunch. Okay, Booker might have been one *big* exception, but he never lost sight of what was important and for most of his long career, he was just a working man who put his job and our bourbon first. He never asked for the limelight, it came to him. I think that attitude permeates the company. At least I'd like to think it does. No matter how big we've gotten, no matter how many countries we're sold in now, no matter how many products we have and sell, at our core we're still that little family-run business starting

out in the foothills on Hardin Creek. Just a Kentucky company doing what we do best, doing what we know. Staying humble can be easier said than done, but getting a big head and starting to believe your own hype leads to complacency, which leads to sloppiness, which leads to mistakes. We've outlasted a lot of competitors and companies because we've never taken anything for granted. Got to work for it, got to get better, every day.

4. *Consistency:* My last point kind of leads into this point. If there's one thing that distinguishes Beam from everyone else, it's our consistency. Over the generations, we've mastered a few things, learned to do them right, and every day we go out and do them. Bourbon making is a process; you can't take shortcuts, can't do one thing one day, one thing the next. Got to do the same thing: every day, every week, every year. So, regardless of what industry you're in, perfect your process, and once you get it right, go out there and do it again and again and again. Be the Master Distiller of your own business, perfect your craft, then share that knowledge with your team and make sure they all understand how important it all is. Make sure they understand that being consistent in what you do is what will separate you from everyone else.

5. *Teamwork:* This might sound a little clichéd, but you need everyone pulling together if you're going to get anywhere. At Beam, we've tried to all get (and

stay) on the same page; it's a priority. Over the years, we've made an effort to ensure that everyone understands where we're going and how we're going to get there. And we've made sure that everyone has a role, from the people in marketing and the sales team out in the field, to the men rolling barrels off a truck. It's all important, it all matters, it all makes a difference. Everyone has to contribute and everyone has to help each other out. Despite our name, we didn't get to where we are because of one man or one family. We got there because of the efforts of thousands of people and dozens of families over hundreds of years. It's been a collective thing. So make sure that your team all understands what the goal is and the strategy you'll use to get there. Then go out there and get it done.

6. *Creating a family:* The people who work for you are more than just employees; they've got problems, hopes, dreams, kids, and parents. In other words, they're people, so you've got to make an effort to understand them and their lives. I think we've done a solid job of doing just that at Beam. We've had people working at our distilleries for years, if not decades. Generations of fathers and sons, even mothers and daughters, more than one husband and wife. There's a reason for that: we've tried to treat them all with respect, we've tried to help them out when we can. We've been firm at times, but hopefully always fair. Once people know that you care about them, once

they feel like they have your respect, they'll be happy, and a happy team is a productive team. It hasn't always been perfect for us, we've had issues over the years, but just like a family, we've worked it out, stayed together, solved the problems. Our company started as a family-run business, and we've made an effort to keep that feeling, maintain that environment.

Family. It's kind of the essence of Beam. It's worked for us, and it can work for you too.

7. *Pride and passion:* You've got to have both of these if you're going to make it. You have to believe in yourself, your product, and your company. You have to believe that you're different, better. And you've got to stand up tall and let your work speak for itself. Be proud of and passionate about what you do. Strive to be the best. More than anything, I think our pride in our bourbon and our passion in making it have sustained us over the years. Our name was, and still is, on the bottle. *We simply could not fail. We simply could not be second best.*

I'll be honest, sometimes when I'm driving down the highway in Kentucky and see one of our trucks with the name "BEAM" written on the side in big, bold letters, I get a lump in my throat, even after all these years. Pride and passion are what they call intangibles. They don't show up in quarterly sales reports, don't show up on any bottom line. But they're both critical, and infectious. If you've got it, chances are someone else on your team will catch it, and chances are it will spread. So keep that head raised high and believe in your work—it will make a difference, maybe even a big one. I know it has for us.

8. *Quality:* I told you most of these were common sense, but you'd be surprised how many companies don't put an emphasis on this, especially nowadays in our "I want it now" culture, when speed and instant gratification are important. There's always a temptation to cut corners, to find ways to water something down to make it cheaper, or to revise the process that has worked for you to make it a little faster. We're a centuries-old company and we've lasted because we've always resisted those temptations. To be sure now, we've innovated, we've added technology, updated things. We don't make whiskey like they did 100 years ago. But we've never skimped on the quality. We know what's important, that what's inside the bottle is what matters.

There have been times when we could have rushed things. A few years back we basically ran out of Knob Creek, one of our Small Batch Bourbons and a big-time seller. Aged nine years at 100 proof. We could have made adjustments, mixed some of our remaining stock with our whiskies, stretched things, or bottled some younger whiskey, but we didn't. The result was a shortage in the marketplace that probably cost us some money, but we didn't rush the process or the whiskey.

When it was ready, we got it back out there. Doing anything else would have compromised our quality. That's not something we do here. And you shouldn't either.

9. *Know your customers:* One more common sense point, but it's important: the customer is king. Repeat after me. There's no reason to go into business if you don't have consumers who will buy what you're selling, so you've got to take care of them. I think we've always done a good job of connecting with the people who buy our products. I've mentioned before that besides making bourbon, the Beams are good at selling it. A lot of that is plain old hard work and relationship building: getting out there and shaking hands, thanking the people, building friendships with the bartenders, the distributors, the restaurant and bar owners, and the general consumers. We don't take anyone for granted, never have. We've always made an effort to let them know we appreciate their loyalty. And we have loyal customers, about as loyal as you can get. People who are engaged with our brand, people who feel part of the Beam family.

Case in point: Not that long ago, we ran a little Facebook promotion. I said if we got more than one million Facebook fans in three months, I would do something bold. (Full disclosure: It was the marketing department's idea, and I went along with it because I didn't think we'd reach the mark, so I thought, what the hell, I'll play along.) Well, I underestimated our customers, underestimated them *big time*. They got into it and we blew by that mark—we added thousands of fans in no time. So, to show my appreciation, and to keep my part of the bargain, I went out and got myself a tattoo of the Jim Beam logo on my arm. It was my first tattoo and it was a big deal because I hate needles, but it was the least I could do, and a deal is a deal. And our customers loved it. I got e-mails from hundreds of them saying they appreciated the effort, appreciated that I kept my word. I also got pictures of other people with Jim Beam tattoos. (Some had gotten them in strange places. . . .) Apparently I wasn't the first one with the idea. So it was all good. I had some fun, but more important, I showed our customers my gratitude. Without them, I'm not sure where I would be. (I'll tell you one thing, I wouldn't be writing a book.) So, stay close to your customers, engage them in your business, and show them you understand them, that you care. I'm not saying you have to go out and get a tattoo, but that might help.

10. *Have a succession plan:* A key reason for our longevity has been our natural succession process. For years we were a family-run business, so passing the mantle was pretty straightforward—the head job was passed down from generation to generation, father to son, or uncle to nephew. In some cases, it was a no-brainer—Jim Beam only had one son, Jere, so that was that. I know that won't and can't work in most other businesses.

That's why you need a plan, need to put some thought into it. Early on, you should identify someone who's eventually going to fill the leadership role and begin grooming him or her. Jacob did that with David and David did that with David M., and so forth down the line. They had a lot of kids, so they had a lot of choices and they chose carefully. (This is all on the distilling side, now; we're not talking about the corporate structure of Beam Inc.)

We already have our eye on my son, Freddie. He's a man now, a college graduate, and he's expressed a keen interest in joining the company. He hasn't yet, and nothing's going to be promised or given to him just because of his bloodline. Also, there won't be any pressure on him to join. Like Booker did with me, it will be his decision. If we open the door, it will be up to him to walk through it. I personally think he has the goods; he's a better student than I was and seems more focused on his future. I'm a little biased, though. I guess time will tell. Regardless, the important thing is that we're already thinking about it, already laying plans so when the time comes, we'll make the right decision, a decision that won't disrupt our business and will keep it moving forward on the right track.

Okay, so there you have it: What Fred Noe Knows about Business. Like I said, no theories about supply and demand, no consumer preference studies, no predictions about trends in the marketplace. Probably won't see this chapter reprinted in the *Harvard Business Review*. But I do know our company, and I do know what built and helped us last. So some advice for you to consider, honest and straightforward, just like my family and just like our bourbons. Use it at your own discretion!

11

HOME

Homeward bound. I looked out the window at the ground below, saw the Ohio River coming into view, shining and snaking through the flat land, curving this way and that. Off in the distance, I saw the knobs in the early evening light, soft sunlight bouncing off of them. Those hills have been there forever, since Jacob Beam's time, and they'll be there long after I'm gone. They've always reminded me of rack houses, strong and sturdy, silently keeping an eye on things, impervious to time.

I don't look out too many windows of airplanes anymore—been on too many flights to pay much attention—but this time I'm glad I did. I had been on the road for three straight weeks, one city after another, the days and nights blending together, everything a blur.

Seeing Kentucky laid out like that down below made me feel good, solid. It also got me thinking about my home state and the business I'm in and how the two are linked together, inseparable.

A few million years ago, an asteroid or meteor or something like that hit the Appalachians in the eastern part of the state, and when it did it helped make Kentucky possible. That thing blew a hole in the mountains and opened up a passageway to the west. The Cumberland Gap, they would eventually call it; a chance for pioneers looking for a better life. People walked through that gap, dragging along their life's possessions behind them in a wooden wagon. Some kept going to other areas, further west to the Mississippi and parts beyond; others stayed forever.

Looking down from the plane, I wondered about the ones who stayed. The ones who made a life in the mountains and in the hills and by the Ohio. I especially thought about the ones who grew corn and turned it into whiskey. A lot of them were kin of mine.

Bourbon and Kentucky have always been one and the same. Can't mention one without mentioning the other. Can't have one without the other. Kentucky made bourbon and bourbon made Kentucky—that's the simple, honest truth.

I've written a lot about the Beams in these pages. I'm proud of my family, proud of what we've done and how long we've done it. But I'm also proud of the whole industry, proud even of our competitors. Over the years we've been through a lot, and I list most of them as good friends: Jimmy Russell and his son Eddie over at Wild Turkey; my cousins, Parker and his son Craig Beam, over at Heaven Hill; Elmer T. Lee at Buffalo Trace; and of course the Samuelses, Bill and Rob, lifelong friends of the Beams, partners and friendly rivals for decades. Even though we're not blood, in a way all of us are.

As I said, the distillers of Kentucky have been through a lot together. First, we had to work to clear the land and protect ourselves against the Indians; later we had to deal with George Washington and the very first tax agents; then came Prohibition and all that it entailed; and finally we had to confront a changing marketplace and the challenges other spirits represented: vodka, scotch, wine, and beer. Our ranks got thinner, but the ones who lasted got stronger. Through it all, we persevered and we helped each other out. If one of us had a problem, we were there: lightning strikes a rack house, you can use one of ours; grain shortage, we'll sell you some corn; distillery flooded, we'll be over with a boat; still breaks down, you can run your whiskey through our pots and columns.

Through the generations, bourbon has bound us together. It's who we are, and it's who we'll always be. In the end, whether you're last name is Beam or not, we're all family, each and every one of us. Just doing what our fathers, our grandfathers, and the men before them taught us.

Bourbon in our blood, bourbon in our bones.

A day or two after I got back from that long trip, I planned a little expedition, an adventure. Years before, Booker had claimed to have found a map that correctly identified the location of Jacob Beam's original well, the spot where he first drew water to make his whiskey. He found the map in the archives of the county courthouse. I didn't believe him; I thought no way that map is for real, no way that well is still out there after two centuries, and if it is, no way we'll find it. But he was insistent that I go search for it; said it was my duty, my responsibility.

Well, I never got around to it, but I kept that map in a safe place and now I dusted it off and was going out after it. I took along Jim the PR guy, and we got in my truck and off we went exploring, in search of the Holy Grail.

We rolled through the hills, Jim squinting at the map and complaining. He wasn't too keen on this idea, thought it was a waste of time, a wild goose chase. But after about 20 wrong turns, we came to a farm in Washington County.

"I think it's over there," I said, pointing. "Past that creek."

We both looked at the map, then back out at the fields in front of us.

"How are we going to get past that creek?" Jim asked.

I opened the door of the truck. "We're walking unless you brought a boat. Come on, Tonto, let's go."

We walked across a flat field, and then we waded through the creek with our shoes still on. It wasn't more than a few inches, but Jim made it seem like we were fording the Amazon.

"You sure about this, Fred?" He kept looking around. I suspect he was thinking about the movie *Deliverance* and a part of me could understand why. We were in the middle of nowhere, deep back country, no one else around. He kept glancing this way and that, a city boy out of his element.

"As long as we don't hear banjo music, we'll be okay." I looked down at the map again. "Straight ahead, I think. Come on. Sun's setting."

We made it across the creek, then through some woods, which opened up to a narrow path. We followed that path around a curve for a bit and there she was: the well.

It was just a hole in the ground, but there were white stones surrounding it to mark its presence. I wasn't sure who had laid down those stones or how long they had been there. I stepped closer to the hole, looked down. It was deep and dark, and after 200 years, that well was dry.

"You sure this is it?" Jim asked.

"Pretty big coincidence if it's not, don't you think? An old map says there's a Jacob's Well out here in Washington County where Jacob lived, and here it is."

We both stared down at the well for a while, and in the late afternoon I thought I could hear my ancestors talking to me, the ghosts whispering.

A few years before, the company had put my likeness on the Jim Beam Bourbon label. It was a surprise, I hadn't expected it, but mostly it was an honor to be listed in such company. Looking into the well, I thought about that now, thought about how I had felt that day when I first saw that bottle, the pride and the emotion that had overwhelmed me. I wish Booker had been around to share those moments. I know he would have been proud as well.

Standing out there in the woods of Washington County, surrounded by the past, I felt a strong connection to my family, especially those other six men on the bottle: Jacob, David, David M., Jim Beam, Uncle Jere, and of course Booker. One family, one bourbon. All Beam.

This whole ride had begun right here for those men, for all of us, at this exact spot. I'm sure that old Jacob had no idea what he was starting when he dropped a bucket down there. Had no idea that we would last this long, or that we would one day be where we are now. From this well to the world.

Seven generations. Maybe one day eight, one after the other, never missing a beat.

"Hey, Fred, you ready?" It was Jim and he was looking at his Blackberry.

"Why don't you go on back?" I said. "I'll be there in a minute."

"You sure? You're going to stay out here all alone? It's getting dark."

"I'll be all right. I'll catch up. Go on now."

So he left, and I just stood there, staring down into that well. It was getting late, but I didn't care. I wanted to stay as long as the light would let me. Besides, I wasn't really alone. My family was there with me, I could feel them all around.

APPENDIX

COCKTAILS

Around the world, people enjoy their bourbon differently. For the most part, I personally like my bourbon straight, with water back. But that's just me. Like I said, everyone has their own preference, their own way of enjoying it. My mom, Annis, she likes her Jim Beam with ginger ale. Booker, he liked it with some water and maybe one single ice cube. It's a personal thing.

One thing is for sure: there's no "proper" way to drink bourbon. It's a very mixable drink, maybe one of the most mixable. So here are a few favorite ways to enjoy it. Some are Beam recipes, some aren't. But they're all good and should be enjoyed responsibly wherever you are in the world.

WHISKEY SOUR

Ingredients:
1½ parts Jim Beam Bourbon
1 part lemon juice
½ tsp. sugar
1 lemon or orange wedge
1 cherry

Preparation:
Add the sugar and the bourbon to the lemon juice. Garnish with lemon or orange wedge and a cherry.

MANHATTAN

Ingredients:
1¾ parts Jim Beam Black
¾ part vermouth
Cherry
Dash of bitters (optional)

Preparation:
Add the sweet vermouth to the bourbon in a Manhattan glass. Optional: add a dash of bitters. Garnish with a cherry.

OLD-FASHIONED

Ingredients:

1½ oz. Jim Beam Bourbon
2 dashes of bitters
Water
Cherry
Orange slice
Lemon wedge
½ tsp. sugar

Preparation:

In an old-fashioned glass, dissolve sugar and bitters in the water. Fill glass with ice. Add bourbon; garnish with cherry, orange slice, and lemon wedge.

BBG (BEAM BLACK AND GINGER ALE)

Ingredients:

1½ parts Jim Beam Black
2 dashes of bitters
4 parts ginger ale
1 lemon wedge

Combine bourbon and bitters in mixer and shake vigorously with no ice. Pour over ice in glass and top with soda. Garnish with lemon wedge.

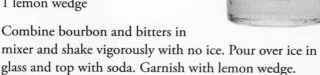

KNOB CREEK BOURBON MINT JULEP

Ingredients:
1½ oz. Knob Creek Bourbon
1 tsp. granulated sugar
2 tsp. water
Finely crushed ice
Fresh mint, washed and
patted dry

Preparation:
In a highball glass, dissolve the
sugar in the water. Fill glass
with crushed ice, and add bourbon. Stir contents until glass
becomes frosty, adding more ice if necessary. Remove stems
from some of the mint leaves and use a straw to push them
into the chilled julep mix for added flavor. Garnish with
remaining sprigs of mint.

THE BITTER DEVIL COCKTAIL

Ingredients:
1 part Devil's Cut Bourbon
1 part ginger ale
1–2 dashes of bitters
1 lemon wedge

Preparation:
Combine ingredients in a rocks glass,
neat or on the rocks. Garnish with
lemon wedge.

DEVIL'S PLAY PUNCH

Ingredients:

1 part Devil's Cut Bourbon

½ part ginger ale

½ part soda water

1 lemon wedge

Preparation:

Combine ingredients in a tall, ice-filled glass.
Garnish with fresh lemon.

RED STAG BREEZE

Ingredients:

1½ parts Red Stag by Jim Beam

3 parts sweet and sour mix

1 part cranberry juice

1 lemon wedge

Preparation:

Combine Red Stag and sweet and sour mix in mixing tin, and
shake vigorously with no ice. Pour over ice in glass and top with
cranberry juice. Garnish with lemon wedge.

SPICED RED TEA

Ingredients:

1½ parts Red Stag by Jim Beam Spiced Bourbon

Hot tea

1 lemon wedge

Preparation:

Build in a heatproof mug. Garnish with a lemon wedge.

HANGOVER CURE

I get asked a lot questions when I'm on the road, but one of the most common, the one I get in just about every city, every country, and every language is, "How can I prevent a hangover?"

Naturally, since it's a primary hazard of my profession, I've done a lot of research on this subject. Over the years, I've consulted with my father, uncles, and cousins, and we all agree that there's only one guaranteed way, one technique, to avoid the Bust Head. It's a bona fide method and it makes a whole lot of sense:

Don't drink too much the night before.

This technique is 100 percent foolproof, guaranteed never to fail.

COOKING WITH BOURBON

Bourbon has been an important part of many recipes for years. My mom, Annis, used it a lot in various dishes. She mostly used Jim Beam, because of the lower proof. Please note: cooking with higher-proof bourbons like Baker's or Booker's can be hazardous to your health. My mom learned that the hard way one night when she was cooking spareribs. She splashed some Booker's on them to marinate them, the closed the oven door. That door didn't stay closed for long; a few minutes later it kicked open—exploded, really—and scared the hell out of us all. A lesson learned: don't cook with 125-proof alcohol!

APPETIZERS

JIM BEAM BBQ DRUMSTICKS

Ingredients

½ cup teriyaki sauce

1 cup oyster sauce

¼ cup soy sauce

¼ cup ketchup

2 tbsp. garlic powder

½ cup Jim Beam Bourbon

2 dashes of liquid smoke flavoring

½ cup white sugar

1½ lb. chicken wings, separated at joints, tips discarded

¼ cup honey

Preparation:

In a large bowl, mix all ingredients except the chicken wings and the honey. Place wings in the bowl, cover, and marinate in the refrigerator 8 hours or overnight. Preheat the grill for low heat. Lightly oil the grill grate. Arrange chicken on the grill and discard the marinade. Grill wings on one side for 20 minutes, then turn and brush with honey. Continue grilling 25 minutes or until juices run clear.

Stuffed Mushrooms with Bourbon

Ingredients
24 medium-sized mushrooms
1 cup melted butter
2 small onions, minced
3 cloves garlic, minced
½ cup parsley, minced
2 tbsp. flour
½ cup seasoned bread crumbs
1 cup sour cream
Salt and pepper, to taste
Jim Beam Bourbon, to drizzle inside mushroom caps and lightly coat the bottom of the baking dish
Parmesan cheese, to taste

Preparation:
Remove and chop mushroom stems. Combine chopped stems with butter, onion, garlic, and parsley. Mix well. Add flour, bread crumbs, sour cream, salt, and pepper. Mix well. Arrange mushroom caps hollow side up in a shallow baking dish, and drizzle a small amount of Jim Beam Bourbon in each cap. Fill caps with stuffing, then sprinkle with parmesan cheese. Add enough bourbon to cover bottom of baking dish. Bake for 20 minutes in 375° oven.

SIDES

BOURBON BAKED BEANS

Ingredients

2 28-oz. cans baked beans

½ cup chili sauce

½ cup strong coffee (best if left over from morning)

¼ cup Jim Beam Bourbon

3 tsp. dry mustard

Preparation:

Combine all ingredients. Pour into a 2-quart casserole dish. Bake at 350° for 1 hour or until good and bubbly.

ENTREES

JIM BEAM BARBECUE SAUCE

Ingredients

2 cups ketchup

4 tbsp. Worcestershire sauce

1 cup Jim Beam Bourbon

4 tbsp. soy sauce

2 tsp. dry mustard

1 cup packed brown sugar

½ tsp. cayenne pepper

4 tbsp. cider vinegar

Preparation:

Combine all ingredients in a medium saucepan. Bring to a boil over high heat, stirring occasionally. Reduce heat to low. Simmer 20–25 minutes, stirring occasionally until thickened. Makes 3–4 cups. Can be stored in refrigerator up to 1 month.

Jim Beam Baby Back Ribs

Ingredients
2 full racks baby back ribs, quartered
1 quart beef broth
2 cups Jim Beam Barbecue Sauce (see recipe, above)
1 cup honey

Preparation:
Place ribs and beef broth in a large, heavy pot or Dutch oven, and add enough water to fully cover ribs. Simmer over low heat for about 1 hour. Once ribs are tender, remove and set aside. Preheat grill to medium heat. Combine barbecue sauce and honey in a medium bowl. Baste ribs generously with sauce and grill for about 4 minutes on each side or until they reach desired degree of doneness.

Steak a la Jim Beam

Ingredients
¼ cup Jim Beam Bourbon
2 tbsp. light sesame oil
2 tsp. Worcestershire sauce
2 one-inch-thick T-bone steaks (or rib-eyes)

Preparation:
Mix first three ingredients well. Place the two steaks into a shallow dish or plate and pour the marinade over the steaks. Cover with plastic wrap and refrigerate at least one

hour prior to grilling. After 30 minutes in the refrigerator, turn the steaks over and allow to marinate for an additional 30 minutes. When the steaks are finished marinating, place the steaks on a hot grill and cook to your satisfaction. Serve your steaks with a tossed salad, baked potatoes, hot rolls, and a refreshing Jim Beam Bourbon and cola.

KNOB CREEK CHICKEN

Ingredients
1 full, boneless chicken breast
1 cup flour
Small amount of cooking oil
4 oz. fresh mushrooms, quartered
Salt, pepper, and garlic powder to taste
1 cup whipping cream (do not whip)
1 tbsp. Knob Creek Bourbon
1 tbsp. beef stock

Preparation:
Flour chicken breast on all sides. Sauté chicken in oil, browning well on both sides. Remove chicken from pan. Add mushrooms and sauté in pan, adding salt, pepper, and garlic powder to taste. Return chicken to pan. Pour whipping cream over chicken. Cook until half of the cream is left or it becomes thick. Add Knob Creek Bourbon and beef stock.

Pork Loin with Knobby Apples and Sweet Onions

Ingredients

1 boneless pork loin roast (preferably center cut), about 3 lb.

2 apples (preferably Honeycrisp or Granny Smith), peeled, cored, and sliced

1 large Maui or other sweet onion, peeled, halved, and sliced

½ tsp. chopped fresh rosemary

2 tbsp. grainy Creole mustard

⅔ cup honey (Tupelo is best, but clover or wildflower is fine)

1 tsp. Asian fish sauce

1 cup plus 2 oz. Knob Creek Bourbon

Salt and cracked pepper to taste

½ lemon, juiced

1 tbsp. butter

1 tbsp. olive oil

Preparation:

Preheat oven to 425°. In a large skillet, heat butter and olive oil over medium heat. Sauté onions for 4–6 minutes, stirring (a little bit of browning is okay). Add apples and continue to cook for 5 more minutes. In the meantime, season pork with salt and cracked pepper, and then rub with grainy mustard and half of the honey. Set pork on a rack and sprinkle with half the rosemary and half the lemon juice. Line a roasting pan with foil to catch juices. Roast pork at 425° for 10 minutes, then lower the heat to 325° and cook for an additional 20 minutes. *Do not open the oven during this process!* Five minutes before the pork is done, remove the apples. Heat apples in a skillet over medium-high heat, and when they start to sizzle, very carefully add 1 cup of Knob Creek Bourbon and flambé. *Be careful of alcohol flames!* After 1 minute, add fish sauce and the remaining lemon juice, honey, and rosemary. Cook together for 2–3 minutes until it has the consistency of a sauce. Add a bit of water if needed to thin sauce a bit. Season with salt and pepper, add lemon, and simmer for 30 seconds. Remove pork from oven and raise heat to 425°. Arrange apples and onions on the roast carefully and pour ¾ of the sauce over it, saving the remaining sauce for later. Put roast back into the oven and bake at 425° for 10 minutes or until the apple-onion topping starts to get slightly browned. Remove roast from oven and pour remaining sauce over it, then let it settle for 10 minutes. Slice and serve with the apples, onions, and pan sauce.

DESSERTS

JIM BEAM BOURBON BALLS

Ingredients
36 pecan halves
4 tbsp. Jim Beam Bourbon
6 tbsp. butter, softened
4 cups confectioners' sugar
Jim Beam Bourbon
½ lb. semi-sweet chocolate

Preparation:
Soak pecan halves in 4 tbsp. Jim Beam Bourbon, 2 hours to overnight. Drain. Drink Jim Beam. Combine butter with confectioners' sugar. Add enough bourbon to make mixture soft enough to roll into balls. Place a pecan half in the center of each ball. Refrigerate. Drink any Jim Beam left over. When bourbon balls are solid, grate chocolate and melt it over lukewarm water. Using a dipping tong or fork, dip each ball into chocolate to coat. Place them in airtight container and store in the refrigerator.

Bread Pudding with Whiskey Sauce

Ingredients
Bread pudding:
1 loaf stale bread, cubed
4 cups milk
2 cups sugar
8 tbsp. melted butter
3 eggs
2 tbsp. vanilla
1 cup raisins
1 cup pecans
1 tsp. nutmeg
Whiskey sauce:
½ cup butter
1½ cup powdered sugar
2 egg yolks
½ cup Jim Beam Bourbon

Preparation:
For bread pudding: Combine all ingredients. Mixture should be very moist but not soupy. Pour into buttered 9- × 13-inch baking dish. Place in preheated 350° oven. Bake for approximately 1 hour and 15 minutes, until top is golden brown. *For whiskey sauce:* Cream butter and sugar over medium heat until all butter is absorbed. Remove from heat and blend in egg yolks. Pour in Jim Beam Bourbon gradually, stirring constantly. Sauce will thicken as it cools. Serve warm over finished bread pudding.

ACKNOWLEDGMENTS

Books don't just happen; they are the result of a lot of work. Fortunately, I had a lot of help, so in no particular order, I would like to thank the following people for their support not only on this project, but in my career as well: Kathleen DiBenedetto, Paula Erickson, Kevin George, Jim Kokoris, Deanna Killackey, Jim Beam Noe, Linda Hayes, Jeff Conder, Matt Shattock, Matt Holt, Shannon Vargo, and Elana Schulman.

Also, special thanks to my family: Sandy, Freddie, and my mom, Annis. For better or worse, you've put up with me for years. Don't think I don't appreciate it.

INDEX

Note: photographs and associated captions are indicated by an italicized I and page number